Emerging Standards for Enhanced Publications and Repository Technology

D1795961

Emerging Standards for Enhanced Publications and Repository Technology

Survey on Technology

Karen Van Godtsenhoven , Mikael Karstensen Elbæk,
Gert Schmeltz Pedersen, Barbara Sierman,
Magchiel Bijsterbosch, Patrick Hochstenbach,
Rosemary Russell, Maurice Vanderfeesten

(Edited by Karen Van Godtsenhoven &
 Marjan Vernooy-Gerritsen)

PART 1:   Introduction
          Karen Van Godtsenhoven

PART 2:   New Technologies and Communities
          Mikael Karstensen Elbaek, Gert Schmeltz Pedersen,
          Barbara Sierman

PART 3:   Framework for Interoperablity
          Magchiel Bijsterbosch, Karen Van Godtsenhoven ,
          Patrick Hochstenbach, Rosemary Russell,
          Maurice Vanderfeesten

AMSTERDAM UNIVERSITY PRESS

This work contains descriptions of the DRIVER II project findings, work and products. In case you believe that this document harms in any way IPR held by you as a person or as a representative of an entity, please do notify us immediately via info@surf.nl. The authors of this document have taken any available measure in order for its content to be accurate, consistent and lawful. However, neither the DRIVER II project consortium as a whole nor the individual partners that implicitly or explicitly participated in the creation and publication of this work hold any sort of responsibility that might occur as a result of using its content. This publication has been produced with the assistance of the European Union. The content of this publication is the sole responsibility of the DRIVER consortium and can in no way be taken to reflect the views of the European Union.

Publisher: Amsterdam University Press, Amsterdam
Cover design: Maedium, Utrecht

ISBN 978 90 8964 189 2 / E-ISBN 978 90 4851 177 8
NUR 953

Trends in Research Information Management

DRIVER studies (2006-2008)

The European Repository Landscape
Maurits van der Graaf & Kwame van Eijndhoven

A DRIVER's Guide to European Repositories
Rene van Horik, Wilma Mossink, Vanessa Proudman, Barbara Sierman, Alma Swan
(Edited by Kasja Weenink, Leo Waaijers & Karen Van Godtsenhoven)

Investigative Study of Standards for Digital Repositories and Related Services
Muriel Foulonneau & Francis André

DRIVER II studies (2008-2009)

The European Repository Landscape 2008
Inventory of Digital Repositories for Research Output in the EU
Maurits van der Graaf
(Edited by Marjan Vernooy-Gerritsen)

Enhanced Publications
Linking Publications and Research Data in Digital Repositories
Saskia Woutersen-Windhouwer, Renze Brandsma, Peter Verhaar,
Arjan Hogenaar, Maarten Hoogerwerf , Paul Doorenbosch, Eugène Dürr,
Jens Ludwig, Birgit Schmidt, Barbara Sierman
(Edited by Marjan Vernooy-Gerritsen)

Emerging Standards for Enhanced Publications and Repository Technology
Survey on Technology
Karen Van Godtsenhoven , Mikael Karstensen Elbæk,
Gert Schmeltz Pedersen, Barbara Sierman, Magchiel Bijsterbosch,
Patrick Hochstenbach, Rosemary Russell, Maurice Vanderfeesten
(Edited by Karen Van Godtsenhoven & Marjan Vernooy-Gerritsen)

Contents

About the contributors 9
About the DRIVER Studies 11
Trends in Research Information Management 13

PART 1.   Introduction 15
1.   On the Structure of this Book 17

PART 2.   New Technologies and Communities 19
2.   Grid computing 21
       2.1   Introduction 21
       2.2   Theory of Grid computing 22
       2.3   Case Studies of Grid computing e-Science 35
       2.4   Opportunities for DRIVER 44
3.   Current Research Information Systems (CRIS) 47
       3.1   Introduction 47
       3.2   Theory of CRIS and digital Repositories 48
       3.3   Case Studies in Ireland, Denmark and The
               Netherlands 60
       3.4   Opportunities for DRIVER 83
4.   Long-term Preservation 85
       4.1   Introduction 85
       4.2   Theory of Long-Term Preservation 85
       4.3   Update on digital Preservation Topics 93
       4.4   Metadata 97
       4.5   Preservation Strategies 98
       4.6   Organisational Aspects of Digital Preservation 100
       4.7   Scientific Data and digital Research Infrastructures 102
       4.8   Opportunities for DRIVER 105

PART 3:   Framework for Interoperablity 107
5.   New Standards, Formats and Evolutions 109
       5.1   Introduction 109
6.   Envelopes and Packages 115
       6.1   Introduction 115
       6.2   Exchanging packaged Information in the Open
               Archive Context 116
       6.3   The Context of Enhanced Publications 119
       6.4   MPEG21-DIDL 121
       6.5   METS 127

6.6   IMS Content Package 131

6.7   ODF Packages 135

6.8   OOXML Open Package Convention 138

6.9   Open eBook Package 142

6.10   Conclusion and Comparison of Package Formats 145

7.   Overlays and Feeds 149

7.1   Introduction 149

7.2   SWAP 149

7.3   ORE, Object Reuse and Exchange 158

7.4   POWDER 170

8.   Embedding 175

8.1   Introduction 175

8.2   Microformats 175

9.   Old and New Publishing Formats 183

9.1.   Introduction 183

9.2   Open Document Format and Office Open XML 183

9.3   CML 186

10.   Web Services 191

10.1   Introduction 191

10.2   Resource-oriented Architecture (ROA) 191

10.3   Service-oriented Architecture 192

References 195

About the contributors

Author

Magchiel Bijsterbosch is Project Coordinator in the SURFshare programme and is responsible for the programme architecture. In DRIVER he has participated in studies on Enhanced Publications object models, interoperability and open standards. In the LOREnet project, Magchiel plays a key role in implementing a national infrastructure for open educational resources. He participates in ongoing studies on impact and requirements for a new national CRIS in The Netherlands.

Mikael Karstensen Elbæk, MLIS holds the position of Systems Librarian and Project Manager of several national and international projects such as the Danish National Research Database, the Danish participation in EU DRIVER II, and the Knowledge Exchange project on Interoperability of OA Repositories and Current Research Information Systems. In addition, he is the chairman of the Danish OA Network, a joint national effort of DEFF and the universities to promote self-archiving, institutional repositories and OA publishing.

Patrick Hochstenbach is Digital Architect at the Ghent University Library. He played a major role in the development of the SFX linking server and cooperated in international standardisation efforts (OpenURL, OAI-PMH, MPEG-21). Currently he is involved in the development of large scale search engines, institutional repository networks and open source projects such as the OAI-PMH Static Repository Gateway. While employed at Los Alamos National Laboratory, he co-authored several publications on the aDORe federated repository framework and developed several of its key components.
Patrick joined this study on 'Emerging Standards for Enhanced Publications and Repository Technology' as technical expert on data interchange formats.

Rosemary Russell works for UKOLN at the University of Bath. She is involved in a range of digital information management projects and initiatives both in the UK and internationally, with a focus on metadata and interoperability issues.

Dr. Gert Schmeltz Pedersen is computer scientist and software developer at DTU Library at the Technical University of Denmark. He has participated in many national and European research and development projects, and he is active in the development and use of the Fedora Commons Repository System.

Barbara Sierman, MA, studied Dutch Literature and started her career in library automation at OCLC-PICA (Pica at that time) in 1979. After that she worked at several IT companies as a consultant. In 2005 she joined the Digital Preservation Department at the Koninklijke Bibliotheek (National Library of the Netherlands), presently holding the position of Digital Preservation Manager. She has written several articles on preservation topics and participates in (international) working groups and projects like Planets and DRIVER.

Maurice Vanderfeesten, MSc is Project Coordinator in the SURFshare program. In DRIVER he participates in studies on Enhanced Publications and related technical trends, interoperability and open standards, and development of demonstrators for depositing, archiving, and harvesting of complex objects in repositories. Maurice plays a key role in defining and implementing the Dutch Scholarly Communication Infrastructure, which include standards, application profiles and support mechanisms for Semantic Web structures, metadata, vocabularies and ontologies, communication protocols, persistent identifier infrastructure for digital objects and authors and global resolution infrastructure for long term retrieval of digital material.

Editors

Karen Van Godtsenhoven , MA studied English Studies, Comparative Literature and Library and Information Sciences. She started working on digital copyright projects for Ghent University Library in 2006, and then became Project Manager for Ghent for DRIVER I and II. Within DRIVER, she is responsible for usability assessment, national networks and advocacy activities. She co-wrote the Interoperability chapter and edited the Technology Watch report in the context of the 'Discovery' work package. She is also editor of the Driver's Guide to European repositories' in DRIVER I. http://dare.uva.nl/aup/nl/record/260224

Dr Marjan Vernooy-Gerritsen is Programme Manager of SURFshare, the programme of the Section ICT and Research of SURFfoundation. The aim of SURFshare is to establish a nationwide infrastructure for sharing research data and information in The Netherlands.

About the DRIVER Studies

The primary objective of the EU funded project *Digital Repositories Infrastructure Vision for European Research*, DRIVER (FP6) and DRIVER II (FP7), was to create a cohesive, robust and flexible, pan-European infrastructure for digital repositories, offering sophisticated services and functionalities for researchers, administrators and the general public. DRIVER's vision was to build a Europe and worldwide Digital Repository infrastructure, which follows the principle of linking users to knowledge.

Today Digital Repositories contain a full spectrum of scholarly materials, from theses, technical reports and working papers to digitised text and image collections. Sometimes they even contain sets of primary research data. Digital repositories may be disciplinary or institutional. In the future, Europe-wide Digital Repository Infrastructure will be a virtual network of physically distributed and peripheral maintained repositories from all countries in Europe. By virtually integrating multiple repositories from many institutions in all European countries, the network will build up a critical mass of research materials, which can be disseminated and presented to the world as a powerful demonstration of research output in Europe. This contributes to innovation in a wide variety of sectors and communities. Within this virtual network, each repository will maintain its own identity and will be clearly marked with a label of the providing repository host.

With the end of the first stage of DRIVER in November 2007, the test bed system D-NET was delivered, producing a search portal with Open Access content from over 70 repositories. DRIVER II moved from a test bed to a production-quality infrastructure and expanded the geographical coverage of Digital Repositories included in it[1].

One of the objectives of DRIVER II was to build a Confederation to promote greater visibility and application of research output through global networks of Open Access digital repositories. This effort led to the launch of the new international organisation COAR, the Confederation of Open Access Repositories in October 2009.

---

[1] http://www.driver-community.eu

DRIVER II significantly broadened the horizon of the whole DRIVER endeavour on infrastructure operation and functionality innovation by state-of-the-art and future-direction studies. After positive appraisal in the mid term review these studies are combined to three reports in the series 'Trends in Research Information Management'[2].

The European Research Repository Landscape 2008 by Maurits van der Graaf is an update of a similar study in 2006. It shows an increasing number of respondents and a further diversification in the character of a repository. These may be institutional or thematically based, and as such non-institutional as well. The ongoing process of widespread and diversification urges coherent approach, as a basic feature of repositories is the retrievability of information that may be dispersed over them. Continued monitoring of developments will be necessary.

Enhanced Publications by Saskia Woutersen-Windhouwer, Renze Brandsma, Peter Verhaar, Arjan Hogenaar, Maarten Hoogerwerf , Paul Doorenbosch, and Eugène Dürr, Ludwig Jens, and Birgit Schmidt is a state-of-the-art overview of the structural elements of an Enhanced Publication, as well as publication models, interrelationship and repository issues. In-depth study is made of object models and functionalities. More practically, a sample is given of datasets together with a demonstrator-project. In the final section, this book deals with long-term preservation issues, linking to the developments of digital repositories that are studied in other books in this series.

Emerging Standards for Enhanced Publications and Repository Technology by Karen Van Godtsenhoven et al. serves as a technology watch on the rapidly evolving world of digital publication. It provides an up-to-date overview of technical issues, underlying the development of universally accessible publications, their elemental components and linked information. More specifically it deals with questions as how to bring together the communities of the Current Research Information Systems (CRIS) and the Common European Research Information Format (CERIF). Case studies like EGEE, DILIGENT and DRIVER are analyzed, as well as implementations in projects in Ireland, Denmark and The Netherlands. Interoperability is the keyword in this context and this book introduces to new standards and to concepts used in the design of envelopes and packages, overlays and feeds, embedding, publishing formats and Web services and service-oriented architecture.

---

[2] http://www.driver-repository.eu

Trends in Research Information Management

Developments in digital data management disclose opportunities never seen before in the world of scientific and scholarly publishing. Research is no longer condensed exclusively in the traditional printed format with its fixed identity as peer reviewed article, journal or book. By losing this traditional identity the single steps in the process of research are becoming accessible as elements that seek context in new relationships. This poses two basic questions for data management: when is an element relevant and what kind of relationship is to be managed.

Data management has inherent questions and problems: uniformity, accessibility, durability and efficiency, to name only a few. Accessibility of the components of the research process will give rise to new ways of collaboration in research. These developments will call for a new approach, Research Information Management.

This series of books are based on trend analyses, an inventory on the scientific repositories in Europe, and state-of-the-art studies in the EU funded DRIVER II project. They are the result of in-depth discussions, troubling with uncertainty about future evolvement, and struggling with the formulation of definitions in the continuously changing world of scholarly communication. Authors, advisors, and reviewers showed perseverance in getting around with the selection of valuable standards and promising developments. I wish to acknowledge all members of the DRIVER community for their contribution to this work.

Choosing the format of a book is a rather traditional starting point that seems appropriate now, as we are only at the beginning of developments. Of course, the content will be presented in other formats as well and naturally in Open Access. And the form of an enriched publication will be pursued, e.g. when theoretical concepts are presented in a mock up or a simulator, as is the case with the 'demonstrators'.

In our series, mixing the format of a book with Internet information occasionally results in pictures of moderate printing quality. We decided not to enhance this part of the publication, but rely on referral to the corresponding Internet site for those who want further reading.

The six DRIVER reports are the beginning of a series of international publications on Trends in Research Information Management (TRIM). The TRIM series will host a variety of publications, mostly offspring of ongoing activities and projects in which SURF participates, written by well-informed authors.

Marjan Vernooy-Gerritsen, editor

Utrecht, September 2009

PART 1. Introduction

Karen Van Godtsenhoven

1. On the Structure of this Book

Parting from a tradition of printed textual publications, the storage of and communication on scientific and scholarly output is rapidly evolving now. So-called 'Enhanced Publications' (EP's), which contain many more data formats, are becoming the next step in this development. An Enhanced Publication is a publication that is enhanced with research data, extra materials, post publication data and database records. It has an object-based structure with explicit links between the objects. An object can be (part of) an article, a data set, an image, a movie, a comment, a module or a link to information in a database.

The authors of this book are fully aware of recent developments in which datasets without an underlying textual publication have been published as journal articles. Hence the above definition of an EP has already changed. However, because we need a workable definition that fits the goals and objectives present discussion in which EP's still are considered to have a textual basis, the choice was made to stick to the above definition throughout this book. It is intended to serve as a useful instrument for D-NET developers and the broader repository community: it is an overview of the new metadata and repository standards as well as the lively communities that use and develop them.

This book consists of two main parts: New Technologies and Communities, and Interoperability. The New Technologies and Communities part contains the following three chapters: one on the Grid, i.e. network, computing community, one on long-term preservation (LTP) strategies and projects, and one on the European CRIS community (Computer Research Information Systems). CRIS-systems are based in research institutions and national administrations, and should evolve into a European-wide e-infrastructure. Of course, there are differences between the repository (publications) and CRIS (research information) communities, but just like Grid computing and LTP, the CRIS community is a related, pan-European community, which deserves a place alongside the other chapters in this publication.

The other part of the book, Interoperability, deals with the new standards, formats and evolutions in the repository world and beyond, all related to the dissemination and interoperability of Enhanced Publications. Forthcoming D-NET developments will need to be interoperable with many of these emerging standards because they are being used to disseminate Enhanced Publications. Every chapter of this part describes an emerging standard, a relevant community or platform, and follows a three-tiered approach: theory, case studies and opportunities for DRIVER. The introduction and theoretical framework explains and defines the technology or community in a DRIVER II context, which is followed by case studies and projects that have implemented these standards or technologies, in order to evaluate the relevance and quality for DRIVER. The last part of every chapter always contains the outcomes for DRIVER II, and serves as input for the technical team for the development of D-NET.

DRIVER partner Technical University of Denmark (DTU) is in charge of both the Grid computing chapter (author Gert Schmeltz Pedersen) and the CRIS chapter (author Mikael Karstensen Elbæk). SURFfoundation in the Netherlands, University of Ghent in Belgium and UKOLN of the University of Bath are partners for the interoperability chapter (authors Maurice Vanderfeesten, Rosemary Russell, Patrick Hochstenbach and Karen Van Godtsenhoven). The Dutch National Library (KB) is responsible for the long-term preservation chapter (author Barbara Sierman).

The expertise of many partners is hence combined, under the auspices of reviewing partners from the University of Bielefeld (Wolfram Horstmann and Friedrich Summann), ICM at the University of Warsaw (Wojtek Sylwestrzak), University of Ghent (Peter Reyniers) and CNR, the National Research Council in Italy (Paolo Manghi).

Because nearly ten authors have written contributions for this book, the chapters all follow their own interpretation of the general three-tiered structure. Although general style and references are respected, it is inevitable that some differences persist.

PART 2. New Technologies and Communities

Mikael Karstensen Elbæk, Gert Schmeltz Pedersen and Barbara Sierman

2. Grid computing

2.1 Introduction

The definition of Grid computing is given in Open Grid Services Architecture Glossary of Terms Version 1.6 (Treadwell, 2007):

> *"A grid is a system that is concerned with the integration, virtualisation, and management of services and resources in a distributed, heterogeneous environment that supports collections of users and resources (virtual organisations) across traditional administrative and organisational domains (real organisations)."*

Grid expertise and experience is already present in DRIVER II, hence the objective of this chapter is to provide the partners involved with a common picture as a basis for further decisions.

The content of this chapter is based on a survey of web-based literature, including Wikipedia[3] and Gridipedia[4], and on participation in the seminar 'Digital Repositories – Interoperability Using Grid Technologies' at the Open Grid Forum conference OGF23[5] (June 2008). Central themes were 'State-of-the-art and future visions', 'User case studies' and 'Key horizontal issues'. Observations from the seminar are the following:

- Listen to the users! But, do not expect them to have any interest in grid technology or in digital repository technology;
- Standardisation activities performed by OGF, Open Grid Forum, resulting in the OGSA, Open Grid Services Architecture recommendations are fundamental Drivers of grid technology;
- Grid technology is very complicated and therefore beyond the reach of the majority of its intended user communities;

---

[3] http://en.wikipedia.org/w/index.php?title=Grid_computing (last access on November 20th, 2008).

[4] http://www.gridipedia.eu (last access on November 20th, 2008).

[5] http://www.ogf.org/gf/event_schedule/index.php?id=1265 (last access on November 20th, 2008).

- Cloud computing is an emerging approach to shared infrastructures, having a lot in common with grid computing, but with less complexity for users;
- The EGEE project with the middleware gLite and the Diligent and D4Science projects with the middleware gCube are success stories despite complexity.

Because of the success story of the EGEE[6], DILIGENT[7] and D4Science[8] projects, these will receive particular focus in the following sections. Furthermore, the DRIVER II "Report on Enhanced Publications: state of the art" from July 2008 and the release of D-NET 1.0 on June 20th, 2008 were also used as input for this chapter.

The chapter starts with an overview of standards and technologies selected as the Grid activities that are deemed most relevant for DRIVER II. These are the standardisation activities performed by OGF, the Open Grid Forum, and published as OGSA, Open Grid Services Architecture recommendations, and by OASIS, published as WSRF, Web Services Resource Framework.

Next, Grid software technology is described, in particular middleware and Grid application development software. We pay attention to emerging cloud computing also. Description of more general software technologies, such as Shibboleth and CAS for security is beyond the scope of the chapter. Then the theoretical approach from the first section will be put in practice, describing use cases of running Grids, in particular EGEE. The third part of this chapter focuses on the evaluation of the importance of the European Grid in the light of DRIVER II, on which the outcomes for the fourth and last section are based.

2.2   Theory of Grid computing

The apparent complexity of Grid computing reflects the mixture of virtual and real organisations in a distributed environment. For a better understanding something should be said on the following concepts and projects.

---

[6] http://www.eu-egee.org (last access on November 20th, 2008).

[7] http://www.diligentproject.org (last access on November 20th, 2008).

[8] http://www.d4science.eu (last access on November 20th, 2008).

2.2.1 OGSA, the Open Grid Services Architecture

The Open Grid Forum (OGF) has embraced the Open Grid Services Architecture (OGSA)[9] as the blueprint for standards-based grid computing. 'Open' refers to the process used to develop standards that achieve interoperability. 'Grid' embodies the integration, virtualisation, and management of services and resources in a distributed, heterogeneous environment. It is 'service-oriented' because it delivers functionality as loosely coupled, interacting services aligned with industry-accepted web service standards. The 'architecture' defines the components, the way in which they are organised and interact and the design philosophy used.

OGSA represents an evolution towards a Grid system architecture based on web services concepts and technologies. Version 1.5 (Foster *et al.*, 2006) defines a set of core capabilities and behaviours that address key concerns in Grid systems. These concerns include issues as how to:
- Establish identity and negotiate authentication;
- Express and negotiate policy;
- Discover services;
- Negotiate and monitor service level agreements;
- Manage membership of, and communication within, virtual organisations;
- Organise service collections hierarchically in order to deliver reliable and scalable service semantics;
- Integrate data resources into computations;
- Monitor and manage collections of services.

The definition of OGSA 1.5 is based on a set of functional and non-functional requirements, which themselves are informed by use cases (see examples in Table 1). The use cases cover infrastructure and application scenarios for both commercial and scientific areas.

Use case	Summary
Commercial Data Center (CDC)	Data centres will have to manage thousands of IT resources, including servers, storage, and networks, while reducing management costs and increasing resource utilisation.

---

[9] http://www.globus.org/ogsa (last access on November 20th, 2008).

Use case	Summary
Severe Storm Modeling	Enable accurate prediction of the exact location of severe storms based on a combination of real-time wide area weather instrumentation and large-scale simulation coupled with data modelling.
Online Media and Entertainment	Delivering an entertainment experience, either for consumption or interaction.
National Fusion Collaboratory (NFC)	Defines a virtual organisation devoted to fusion research and addresses the needs of software developed and executed by this community based on the application service provider (ASP) model.
Service-Based Distributed Query Processing	A service-based distributed query processor supporting the evaluation of queries expressed in a declarative language over one or more existing services.
Grid Workflow	Workflow is a convenient way of constructing new services by composing existing services. A new service can be created and used by registering a workflow definition to a workflow engine.
Grid Resource Reseller	Inserting a supply chain between the Grid resource owners and end users will allow the resource owners to concentrate on their core competences, while end users can purchase resources bundled into attractive packages by the reseller.
Inter Grid	Extends the CDC use case by emphasizing the plethora of applications that are not Grid-enabled and are difficult to change, e.g. mixed Grid and non-Grid data centers, and Grids across multiple companies. Also brings into view generic concepts of utility computing.
Interactive Grids	Compared to the online media use case, this use case emphasises a high granularity of distributed execution.
Grid Lite	Extends the use of grids to small devices—PDAs, cell phones, firewalls, etcetera.—and identifies a set of essential services that enable the device to be part of a grid environment.

Use case	Summary
Virtual Organization (VO) Grid Portal	A VO gives its members access to various computational, instrument-based data and other types of resources. A Grid portal provides an end-user view of the collected resources available to the members of the VO.
Persistent Archive	Preservation environments handle technology evolution by providing appropriate abstraction layers to manage mappings between old and new protocols, software and hardware systems, while maintaining authentic records.
Mutual Authorization	Refines the CDC and NFC use cases by introducing the additional requirement of the job submitter authorizing the resource on which the job will eventually execute.
Resource Usage Service	Facilitates the mediation of resource usage metrics produced by applications, middleware, operating systems, and physical (computer and network) resources in a distributed, heterogeneous environment.

Table 1. Some OGSA Use Cases

OGSA should enable interoperability between diverse, heterogeneous, and distributed resources and services, as well as reduce the complexity of administering heterogeneous systems. Many functions required in distributed environments, such as security and resource management, may already be implemented in stable and reliable legacy systems. It will rarely be feasible to replace such legacy systems that are often old. Instead, they must be integrated into the Grid.

The need to support heterogeneous systems leads to requirements that include the following:

- *Resource Virtualisation.* Essential to reduce the complexity of managing heterogeneous systems and to handle diverse resources in a unified way.

- *Common Management Capabilities.* Simplifying administration of a heterogeneous system requires mechanisms for uniform and consistent management of resources. A minimum set of common manageability capabilities is required.

- *Resource Discovery and Query.* Mechanisms are required for discovering resources with desired attributes and for retrieving their properties. Discovery and query should handle a highly dynamic and heterogeneous system.

- *Standard Protocols and Schemes.* Important for interoperability. Standard protocols are also particularly important as their use can simplify the transition to using Grids.

- *Global name space.* To ease data and resource access. OGSA entities should be able to access other OGSA entities transparently, subject to security constraints, without regard to location or replication.

- *Metadata Services.* Important for finding, invoking, and tracking entities. It should be possible to allow for access to and propagation, aggregation, and management of entity metadata across administrative domains.

- *Site Autonomy.* Mechanisms are required for accessing resources across sites while respecting local control and policy.

- *Resource Usage Data.* Mechanisms and standard schemas for collecting and exchanging resource usage, i.e. consumption, data across organisations, for the purpose of e.g. accounting and billing.

- *Support for various Job Types.* Execution of various types of jobs must be supported including simple jobs and complex jobs such as workflow and composite services.

- *Job Management.* It is essential to be able to manage jobs during their entire lifetimes. Jobs must support manageability interfaces and these interfaces must work with various types of groupings of jobs, e.g. workflows and job arrays. Mechanisms are also required for controlling the execution of individual job steps as well as orchestration or choreography services.

- *Scheduling.* The ability to schedule and execute jobs based on such information as specified priority and current allocation of resources is required. It is also required to realise mechanisms for scheduling across administrative domains, using multiple schedulers.

- *Resource Provisioning.* To automate the complicated process of resource allocation, deployment, and configuration. It must be possible to deploy the required applications and data to resources and configure them automatically, if necessary deploying and re-configuring hosting environments such as OS and middleware to prepare the environment needed for job execution. It must be possible to provision any type of resource, not just compute resources, but, for example, network or data resources.

The OGSA services framework is shown in Figure 1. In the figure, cylinders represent individual services. The services are built on web service standards, with semantics, additions, extensions and modifications that are relevant to grids.

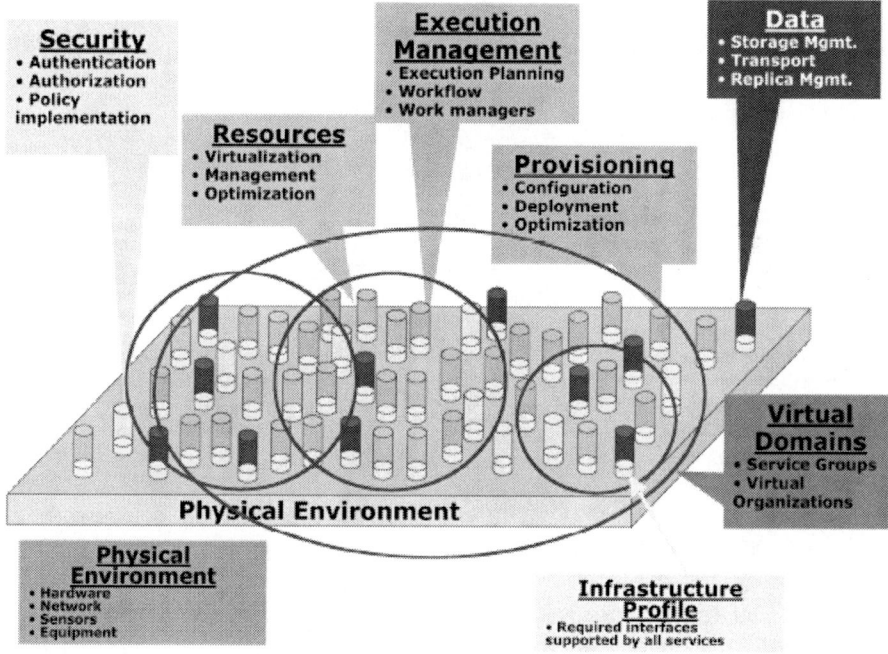

Figure 1. The OGSA Services Framework

The OGSA Roadmap (Jordan and Kishimoto, 2008) provides an overview of the many interrelated recommendations and informational documents being produced by the OGSA and related working groups. OGSA software adheres to OGSA normative specifications and profiles, and thus enables customers to deploy Grid solutions that interoperate even when based on different open-source or commercial software vendors' implementations.

Figure 2 shows the structure of whole OGSA documents, especially the relationship among high-level informational documents, profiles, and actual normative specifications. The Open Grid Services Infrastructure (OGSI) is related to OGSA, as it was originally intended to form the basic 'plumbing' layer for OGSA. It has been superseded by WSRF and WS-Management.

GridForge[10] represents the main collaboration toolkit used by the OGF community, to share documents and meeting materials, and to collaboratively work on OGF standards.

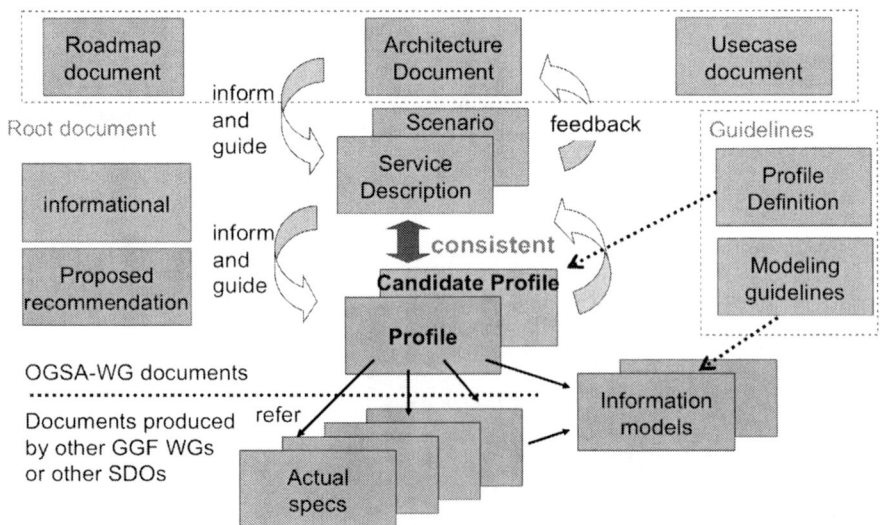

Figure 2. OGSA documents and their structure

2.2.2   Web Services Resource Framework (WSRF)

The purpose of the Web Services Resource Framework[11] (WSRF) is to define a generic framework for modelling and accessing persistent

---

[10] http://forge.ogf.org/sf/sfmain/do/home (last access on November 20th, 2008).

resources using web services to simplify the definition and implementation of a service and the integration and management of multiple services.

The OASIS organisation has developed five specifications for WSRF, i.e. WS-Resource, WS-ResourceProperties, WS-ResourceLifetime, WS-ServiceGroup, and WS-BaseFaults. Together and with the WS-Notification specification, these specifications facilitate implementation of OGSA capabilities using web services. WSRF is considered to be the real interoperability platform for Grid middleware.

2.2.3 Grid Middleware

Grid middleware is software that is layered between the application software and the underlying hardware and its software services (see Table 2).

Name	Description
gLite[12]	LightWeight Middleware for Grid Computing.
	The gLite distribution is an integrated set of components designed to enable resource sharing. In other words, this is middleware for building a Grid.
	The gLite middleware is produced by the EGEE project. In addition to code developed within the project, the gLite distribution pulls together contributions from many other projects, including LCG. The distribution model is to construct different services ('node-types') from these components and then ensure easy installation and configuration on the chosen platforms (currently Scientific Linux versions 3 and 4).
	gLite middleware is currently deployed on hundreds of sites as part of the EGEE project and enables global science in a number of disciplines, notably serving the LCG project.

---

[11]http://www.oasis-open.org/committees/tc_home.php?wg_abbrev=wsrf (last access on November 20th, 2008).

[12] http://glite.web.cern.ch/glite (last access on November 20th, 2008).

Name	Description
gCube[13]	gCube enables scientists to build transient Virtual Research Environments (VREs) declaratively and dynamically by aggregating and deploying on-demand content resources, application services, and computing resources. It also monitors the shared resources during the VREs lifetime guaranteeing optimal allocation and exploitation. Finally, it provides mechanisms for creating VREs-dedicated web portals, through which scientists can access their content and services easily.

The gCube system is realised as a service oriented framework composed of a set of interacting services, providing:

• support for creating and operating on-demand transient virtual research environment;

• features necessary for handling shared content and application resources;

• access to information sources and applications provided by third-parties;

• a set of typical DL functions, like search, annotation, personalisation, document visualisation.

These services are designed to exploit the gLite middleware and are capable to consume the high computational and storage capabilities of the Grid infrastructure released by the EGEE project. Thus, gCube services support complex and time consuming functionalities, while focusing on optimizing resource usage and satisfying QoS contracts. gCube exploits WSRF together with WS-Notification, WS-Addressing, and WS-Security. |
| Globus Toolkit[14] | The open source Globus® Toolkit is a fundamental enabling technology for the Grid, letting people share computing power, databases, and other tools securely online across corporate, institutional, and geographic boundaries without sacrificing local autonomy. |

---

[13] http://www.gcube-system.org (last access on November 20th, 2008).
[14] http://www.globus.org/toolkit (last access on November 20th, 2008).

Name	Description
	The Globus® toolkit includes software services and libraries for resource monitoring, discovery, and management, plus security and file management. In addition to being a central part of science and engineering projects that total nearly a half-billion dollars internationally, the Globus Toolkit is a substrate on which leading IT companies are building significant commercial Grid products.
	The toolkit includes software for security, information infrastructure, resource management, data management, communication, fault detection, and portability. It is packaged as a set of components that can be used either independently or together to develop applications. Every organisation has unique modes of operation, and collaboration between multiple organisations is hindered by incompatibility of resources such as data archives, computers, and networks. The Globus Toolkit was conceived to remove obstacles that prevent seamless collaboration. Its core services, interfaces and protocols allow users to access remote resources as if they were located within their own machine room while simultaneously preserving local control over who can use resources and when.
	The Globus Toolkit 4.0 and later versions provide an open source WSRF development kit and a set of WSRF services.
UNICORE[15]	UNICORE (Uniform Interface to Computing Resources) offers a ready-to-run Grid system including client and server software. UNICORE has special characteristics that make it unique among Grid middleware systems. The

UNICORE design is based on several guiding principles that serve as key objectives for further enhancements: |

---

[15] http://www.unicore.eu (last access on November 20th, 2008).

Name	Description
	• *Abstraction.* UNICORE users don not need to know details about the system that they use. UNICORE provides abstractions for concepts such as application software and storage locations. Thus, UNICORE allows seamless access to heterogeneous environments.
	• *Security.* UNICORE offers strong security based on industry standards such as the X.509 PKI. Communication over the internet is protected by mutual authentication. The UNICORE security concept includes Explicit Trust Delegation (Snelling *et al.*, 2004) and novel VO management based on XSAML[16].
	• *Site autonomy.* When making resources available on the Grid, administrators keep fine-grained control about their resources. Local policies are respected.
	• *Ease of use.* A powerful GUI client covers the most common usage scenarios, such as application execution and multi-step, multi-site workflows.
	UNICORE 6 is using WSRF and can be considered as fully compliant with WSRF.
ARC[17] - Advanced Resource Connector	ARC provides a reliable implementation of the fundamental Grid services, such as information services, resource discovery and monitoring, job submission and management, brokering and data management and resource management. The middleware builds upon standard Open Source solutions like the OpenLDAP, OpenSSL, SASL and Globus Toolkit® (GT) libraries. ARC is much more than a Globus Toolkit; it is an out-of-the-box Grid solution that offers its own services built upon the GT libraries. The ARC middleware is deployed and used in the NorduGrid production environment.

Table 2. Grid middleware

---

[16] http://sourceforge.net/project/showfiles.php?group_id=159625&-package_id=211108 (last access on November 20th, 2008).

[17] http://www.nordugrid.org/middleware (last access on November 20th, 2008).

2.2.4 Gridification or Grid-enabling of Applications

Software and/or methods for the construction of applications that may run on a Grid is contained in Table 3.

Name	Description
g-Eclipse [18]	The g-Eclipse project aims to build an integrated workbench framework to access the power of existing Grid infrastructures. The framework will be built on top of the reliable eco-system of the Eclipse community to enable a sustainable development. The framework will provide tools to customise Grid users' applications, to manage Grid resources and to support the development cycle of new Grid applications. Therefore, already existing tools (such as the Migrating Desktop, the GridBench suite, and the Grid Visualisation Kernel (GVK)) will be integrated. The project will aim for general Grid workbench tools that can be extended for many different Grid middleware's (such as gLite, UNICORE, Globus toolkit), starting with implementations for the gLite middleware
GRID superscalar [19]	GRID superscalar is a new programming paradigm for Grid-enabling applications, composed of an interface and a run-time. With GRID superscalar, a sequential application composed of tasks of certain granularity is automatically converted into a parallel application where the tasks are executed in different servers of a computational Grid. The aim of GRID superscalar is to reduce the development complexity of grid applications to a minimum, in such a way that writing an application for a computational grid may be as easy as writing a sequential application.
Intel's Grid Programming Environment[20]	Intel's Grid Programming Environment is an Open Source technology demonstrator that provides a full Grid software stack ready to be used out-of-the-box. It

---

[18] http://www.eclipse.org/geclipse (last access on November 20th, 2008).

[19] http://www.bsc.es/plantillaG.php?cat_id=69 (last access on November 20th, 2008).

Name	Description
	enables the development of Grid–enabled applications that are independent of the underlying Grid middleware, and includes powerful graphical user interfaces for Grid experts, administrators and end users.

Table 3. Gridification or Grid-enabling of applications

2.2.5 Cloud Computing

Cloud computing is an emerging approach to shared infrastructure in which large pools of systems are linked together to provide IT services. A specific example is Amazon EC2, Elastic Compute Cloud[21].

Amazon EC2's web service interface allows to obtain and configure capacity, scaling up and down as computing requirements change, paying only for capacity used. Amazon EC2 provides developers the tools to upload custom Amazon Machine Image (AMI) into Amazon S3, Simple Storage Service, manage access permissions, and run the image using as many or few systems as desired.

A comparative study of Grids and Clouds (Bégin *et al.*, 2008) was presented at OGF23 (Bégin, 2008). Clouds and Grids do have a lot in common, but there are differences. One important difference is that Grids are typically used for job execution. Job execution is limited duration execution of a programme, often as part of a larger set of jobs, consuming or producing all together a significant amount of data. Clouds are more often used to support long-serving services. Users are gaining confidence in the cloud services and are now outsourcing production services and part of their IT infrastructure to cloud providers such as Amazon. Grids provide higher-level services that are not covered by clouds. Those are services enabling complex distributed scientific collaborations, i.e. virtual organisations, in order to share computing, data and ultimately scientific discoveries.

A related development is the Google App Engine[22], also called Google Cloud. Computing infrastructure is rapidly turning into a utility and Google App Engine is yet another example of this.

---

[20] See Intel (2006), in references (Grid section).

[21] http://www.amazon.com/gp/browse.html?node=3435361 (last access on November 20th, 2008).

2.3　Case Studies of Grid computing e-Science

2.3.1　EGEE

Enabling Grids for E-sciencE (EGEE and EGEE-III) is the largest multi-disciplinary Grid infrastructure in the world, bringing together more than 120 organisations to produce a reliable and scalable computing resource available to the European and global research community.

EGEE is providing a production quality Grid infrastructure spanning about 50 countries with over 250 sites to a myriad of applications from various scientific domains, including Earth Sciences, High Energy Physics, Bioinformatics and Astrophysics.

The EGEE Grid infrastructure consists of a set of middleware services deployed on a worldwide collection of computational resources. It provides three services to users:

- *Production Service.* This is the largest Grid infrastructure provided by EGEE. It runs the latest stable version of the gLite middleware. This is the preferred service for large-scale, production use of the Grid.

- *Preproduction Service.* This consists of a limited number of sites running a preview of the next release of the gLite software. This should be used to test existing applications against new releases and to understand new gLite services.

- *GILDA t-infrastructure.* This is a Grid that runs the entire gLite software stack in parallel to the Production and Preproduction Services. It is used to demonstrate EGEE grid technology and to support training courses.

2.3.2　DILIGENT

The main objective of DILIGENT has been to create an advanced test bed for knowledge e-Infrastructure that will enable members of dynamic virtual e-Science organisations to access shared knowledge and to collaborate in a secure, coordinated, dynamic and cost-effective way. It is built by integrating Grid and digital library technology. The merging of these two technologies opened the way to a new generation

---

[22] http://appengine.google.com (last access on November 20th, 2008).

of e-Science knowledge e-Infrastructures able to provide powerful environments for research and industrial applications.

DILIGENT has released the gCube system version 1.0, which is the foundation infrastructure on which DILIGENT will provide on-demand digital libraries to dynamic virtual organisations by exploiting the high-computing capacities of the Grid. From a logical point of view, the gCube system is organised in layers (see Figure 3).

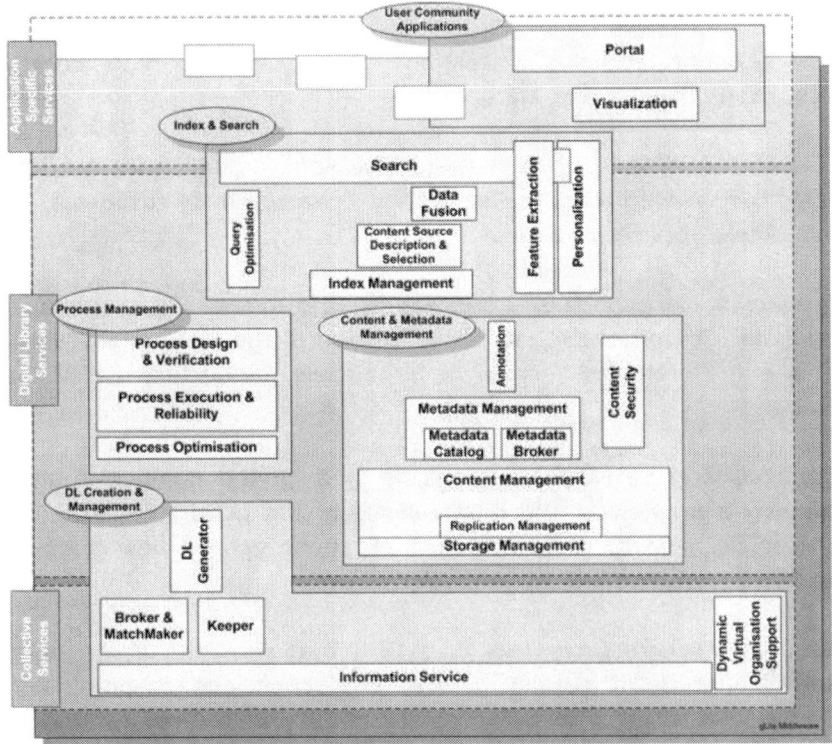

Figure 3. gCube system layers

The Collective Layer

The Collective Layer enhances existing Grid collective services with the functionalities able to support the complex services interactions required by the Digital Library Layer. The Collective Layer contains services that are not associated with any one specific resource but are rather global in nature and manage interactions across collections of resources.

The Digital Library Layer

The Digital Library Layer selects, integrates and enhances a set of reliable and dependable production-quality services, developed in digital library projects and applications, in order to cover the, indexing and discovery of mixed-media objects like documents, videos, images, and environmental data, and the management and processing of these objects through annotation, composition, and cooperative editing. It also supports the dynamic creation and access to transient virtual research environment. fundamental functionalities required for any virtual research environment in the e-knowledge area. The services of this layer provide submission

The Application Specific Layer

The Application Specific Layer contains application specific services. Third-party providers are enabled to migrate their data or functional components to the gCube framework. Specifications are being produced that facilitate the plug-in of legacy components needed to support user-specific scenarios and enable the reuse of existing content and applications.

2.3.3 DRIVER-related Grid Activities

Table 4 lists DRIVER-related Grid activities that may be interesting for this study, and which were not already covered in the sections above. It states their relevance for DRIVER-Grid interaction and mentions involvement of DRIVER partners in the activities.

Activity name	Activity type	Activity title or description	DRIVER partner in-volved	Relevance for DRIVER-Grid inter-action
BEinGRID D[23]	FP6 project	Business Experiments in GRID.	CNR, NKUA	Examples in many appli-cation areas
BELIEF-II[24]	FP7 project	Bringing Europe's eLectronic Infrastructures to Expanding Frontiers.	CNR, NKUA	Example of a digital library using GÉANT

---

[23] http://www.beingrid.eu (last access on November 20th, 2008).

[24] http://www.beliefproject.org (last access on November 20th, 2008).

Activity name	Activity type	Activity title or description	DRIVER partner in-volved	Relevance for DRIVER-Grid inter-action
Chemo-mentum [25]	FP6 project	Grid Services based Environ-ment to enable Innovative Research.	ICM	Example of service develop-ment
Core-GRID [26]	FP6 Network of Excel-lence	The European Research Net-work on Foundations, Soft-ware Infrastructures and Applications for large scale distributed, GRID and Peer-to-Peer Technologies.	CNR	Knowledge about de-velopment of next generation grid mid-dleware
D4-Science [27]	FP7 project	D4Science stands for **DI**stributed col**L**aboratories **I**nfrastructure on **G**rid **EN**-abled **T**echnology (DILIGENT) **4 Science**	CNR, NKUA	Closely re-lated, may be attached as ad-vanced DR
DARIAH [28]	FP7 project	Digital Research Infrastruc-ture for the Arts and Humanities. The digital research infra-structure will integrate grid middleware with user facing tools to support e-research and e-learning activities.	UGOE	Should be followed as example within hu-manities
DEISA / DEISA2 [29]	FP6+7 projects	Distributed European Infra-structure for Supercomput-ing Applications.	CNRS	Example Grid

[25] http://www.chemomentum.org/c9m (last access on November 20th, 2008).

[26] http://www.coregrid.net (last access on November 20th, 2008).

[27] http://www.d4science.eu (last access on November 20th, 2008).

[28] http://www.dariah.eu (last access on November 20th, 2008).

[29] http://www.deisa.eu (last access on November 20th, 2008).

Activity name	Activity type	Activity title or description	DRIVER partner in-volved	Relevance for DRIVER-Grid inter-action
D-Grid[30]	National initiative to establish a grid infra-structure for Germany	Developing a distributed, integrated resource platform for high-performance com-putting and related services.		Examples in many appli-cation areas
DReSNet [31]	EPSRC project	Digital Repositories in e-Science Network The proposed Network is motivated by the potential for synergy between two fields of technology and technique, e-Science and Digital Repositories, and the benefits that will be obtained by increasing interaction and cooperation between re-searchers and practitioners in these fields. (EPSRC, Engineering and Physical Sciences Research Council, is the UK Govern-ment's leading funding agency for research and training in engineering and the physical sciences).		Should be followed

---

[30] http://www.d-grid.de (last access on November 20th, 2008).

[31] http://www.dresnet.net (last access on November 20th, 2008).

Activity name	Activity type	Activity title or description	DRIVER partner involved	Relevance for DRIVER-Grid interaction
e-SciDR[32]	FP6 study	e-SciDR is a study to drive forward the development and use of digital repositories in the EU in all areas of science, from the humanities to the earth sciences.		The study aims to provide the European Commission with an overview of the situation in Europe
EGI_DS [33]	FP7 project	European Grid Initiative (EGI) Design Study Towards a sustainable production Grid infrastructure.	CNRS	Evaluating use cases
GÉANT2 [34]	GÉANT2 is co-funded by the EC and Europe's national research and education networks	GÉANT2 is the seventh generation of pan-European research and education network, successor to the pan-European multi-gigabit research network GÉANT. The GÉANT2 network connects 34 countries through 30 national research and education networks		Used by EGEE
Health-e-Child[35]		An integrated platform for European pediatrics based on a Grid-enabled network of leading clinical centres	NKUA	Example application

---

[32] http://www.e-scidr.eu (last access on November 20th, 2008).

[33] http://web.eu-egi.eu (last access on November 20th, 2008).

[34] http://www.geant2.net (last access on November 20th, 2008).

[35] http://www.health-e-child.org (last access on November 20th, 2008).

Activity name	Activity type	Activity title or description	DRIVER partner in-volved	Relevance for DRIVER-Grid inter-action
KnowARC [36]	FP6 project	Grid-enabled Know-how Sharing Technology Based on ARC Services and Open Standards. The KnowARC project aspires to improve and extend the existing state-of-the-art technology found in the Advanced Resource Con-nector (ARC) middleware, which provides a set of reli-able, robust, non-intrusive, well-tested core services.		Should be followed
Next GRID [37]	FP6 project	Architecture for Next Generation Grids.	CNR, NKUA	Architec-tural input
NGG [38]	FP6 Next Genera-tion Grid (NGG) Expert Group	"Future for European Grids: GRIDs and Service Oriented Knowledge Utilities", January 2006, outlines vision and research directions 2010 and beyond.	CNR, NKUA	Vision and research directions

---

[36] http://www.knowarc.eu (last access on November 20th, 2008).

[37] http://www.nextgrid.org (last access on November 20th, 2008).

[38] http://cordis.europa.eu/ist/grids/ngg.htm (last access on November 20th, 2008).

Activity name	Activity type	Activity title or description	DRIVER partner in-volved	Relevance for DRIVER-Grid inter-action
Nordic Data Grid Facility, NDGF[39]	The Nordic Data Grid Facility, NDGF, is a col-labora-tion be-tween the Nordic coun-tries.	The motivation for NDGF is to ensure that researchers in the Nordic countries can create and participate in computational challenges of scope and size unreachable for the national research groups alone. NDGF is a *production grid* facility that leverages exist-ing, national computational resources and grid infra-structures. Currently, several Nordic resources are accessible with ARC and gLite grid middle-ware, some sites with both. (Nordic countries are Den-mark, Finland, Norway, Sweden).		May provide example Grid ser-vices
Nordu-Grid[40]	Nordu-Grid is a Grid Research and Develop ment col-labora-tion	The aim of the NorduGrid collaboration is to deliver a robust, scalable, portable and fully featured solution for a global computational and data Grid system. NorduGrid develops and deploys the ARC middleware.		ARC mid-dleware is a candidate for interac-tion

---

[39] http://www.ndgf.org/ndgfweb/home.html (last access on November 20th, 2008).

[40] http://www.nordugrid.org (last access on November 20th, 2008).

Activity name	Activity type	Activity title or description	DRIVER partner in-volved	Relevance for DRIVER-Grid inter-action
OMII-Europe[41]	FP6 project OMII = Open Middle-ware Infra-structure Institute	OMII-Europe will develop a repository of quality-assured Grid services running on existing major Grid infra-structures. The OMII-Europe goals are interoperability, quality-assurance and to establish itself as an impartial broker, giving advice on het-erogeneous Grid solutions.		May de-velop rele-vant ser-vices
TextGrid [42]	Project part of D-Grid	Modular platform for collabo-rative textual editing, a community Grid for the humanities.	UGOE	Example
UniGrids [43]	FP6 project	Uniform Interface to Grid Services. The UniGrids project will de-velop a Grid Service infra-structure compliant with the Open Grid Service Architec-ture (OGSA). It is based on the UNICORE Grid software initially developed in the German UNICORE and UNICORE Plus projects.	ICM	Candidate for Grid interaction

Table 4. DRIVER-related Grid activities (sorted by activity name)

---

[41] http://omii-europe.org (last access on November 20th, 2008).

[42] http://www.textgrid.de (last access on November 20th, 2008).

[43] http://www.unigrids.org (last access on November 20th, 2008).

2.4 Opportunities for DRIVER

Grid technology is very complicated and as such not directly applicable by the majority of its intended user communities. Current development trends, in order to simplify and/or hide complexity, are:
- Community-specific user interfaces, as in D4Science;
- Functionality for creating Enhanced Publications or "Scientific Publication Packages", where Grid resources are included in publications with less pain;
- Scholarly workbenches, like eSciDoc;
- Cloud computing.

There are also considerable successes for Grid technology, despite complexity:
- EGEE with gLite;
- DILIGENT with gCore;
- The Grid concept of virtual organisations is fruitful for driving interoperation of digital repositories.

So, recommendations from this study are:
- DRIVER/D-NET should be able to interoperate with OGSA-based middleware in order to support Enhanced Publications with linkage of Grid-based resources;
- DRIVER/D-NET should be able to interoperate with OGSA-based middleware in order to exploit Grids, by utilizing storage elements for selective replication, and by utilizing compute elements for heavy computing tasks;
- DRIVER/D-NET should implement functionality and user interfaces for creating and maintaining Enhanced Publications;
- DRIVER II should follow the evolution of scholarly workbenches;
- DRIVER II has to follow the evolution of cloud computing services in order to become ready to interoperate;
- DRIVER could benefit from mediator services providing DRIVER services with access to Grid infrastructures. Infrastructures could be either service-oriented or job-oriented, depending on the functional and computational needs of the DRIVER services. For example, if DRIVER will be endowed with services capable of analyzing large quantities of full-texts (millions) to extract statistics or information, the computational needs would go well beyond those available to individual machines on the DRIVER network and an interface to the job-oriented grid could solve the problem.

Finally, we quote a recent viewpoint on Grid technology by Wolfgang Gentzsch (DEISA Duke University):

> *"It looks like we have to say goodbye to our good, old Grids of the past at least to all those beautiful features and capabilities envisioned 10 years ago, when Grids were supposed to evolve toward coordinated resource sharing and problem solving in dynamic, multi-institutional virtual organisations, and even to extend beyond their scientific scope. This is a great vision, but it is becoming more and more obvious that in order to make it happen, we need much more time and effort than originally anticipated." … "The good news is that clouds will help Grids to survive. They teach Grids that in order to be widely accepted and thus sustainable, they have to be simple, user-friendly, service-oriented, scalable, on-demand, SLA-driven, with simple APIs, and so on just like clouds." (Gentzsch, 2008).*

3. Current Research Information Systems (CRIS)

3.1 Introduction

Current Research Information Systems (CRIS) are receiving increasing attention in Europe these years. Global research is becoming more and more competitive, which increases the need for systematic management of research. At the same time, digital repositories, whether they are institutional repositories or subject repositories, obtained a 'critical mass' (Van der Graaf, Van Eijndhoven, 2008). Most universities have an institutional repository where researchers can archive their publications and the results from their research.

CRIS's are traditionally implemented and managed by research administrations at universities, which are mainly referring to context of research, or the description thereof, whereas digital repositories are referring to the content of research, i.e. full-texts (Razum *et al.*, 2007). The two information domains outline what could be dubbed the Academic Information Domain. The synergy between the two information domains is interesting for the DRIVER community because evidence show that well populated repositories are backed by CRIS's (Rusbridge, 2008).

With two systems that are traditionally managed and implemented by two different organisational units, but covering similar information and concerning the same people, the risk of building information silos and duplicated work is evident. One of the biggest motivations of discovering the correlation between CRIS and repositories is the synergies that are obtainable and eliminate redundant work.

This chapter will provide an insight into the basics of Current Research Information Systems as it relates more and more to the domain of digital repositories (DR). It will also introduce the leading standardisation of the CRIS data model Current European Research Information Format (CERIF) and the community behind it, EuroCRIS. Three different case studies will demonstrate different uses and synergies of CRIS's and institutional repositories (IR) in The Netherlands, Ireland and Denmark. Finally, the chapter will deal with the implications for the DRIVER infrastructure of becoming interoperable with CRIS-systems.

3.2   Theory of CRIS and digital Repositories

In the *Strand Report of the Knowledge Exchange Institutional Repository Workshop on Echanging Research Information*, the concept of the Academic Information Domain (AID) was introduced (Razum, M. et al. 2007:3). The model is a simplification of the overall setting of information supply and management of academic institutions. The model distinguishes between information elements, i.e. entities and attributes, which are mostly related to the academic information processes in research and education, and those that are more related to the administration of the university. The simple model contains the Personnel Information Domain (LDAP/HR-systems), Financial Information Domain (ERP) and finally, the Academic Information Domain (CRIS and Digital Repositories) where the CRIS is overlapping the domains of Personnel and Financial Information Domains.

Overview of typical systems within the overlapping information domains of AID:

- *Personnel Information Domain.* Human Resource Management System and LDAP directory service for looking up information about employees;

- *Financial Information Domain.* Enterprise Resource Planning systems (ERP) and Project management systems.

- *Academic Information Domain.* Current Research Information Systems, and Open Access Repositories, such as Institutional Repositories, and Learning Management Systems.

- *Enterprise Content Management Domain.* Content Management Systems and Electronic Records/Document Management Systems.

The AID was later enhanced by Chris Baars *et al.* (2008) to also contain E-research, i.e. datasets, as was shown in several presentations of the Dutch national research portal NARCIS. The model presented here is based on the previous models of the AID but has been extended with Enterprise Content Management Domain and the AID has been extended with Learning Management Systems (LMS), thus attempting to capture the AID at a more comprehensive level.

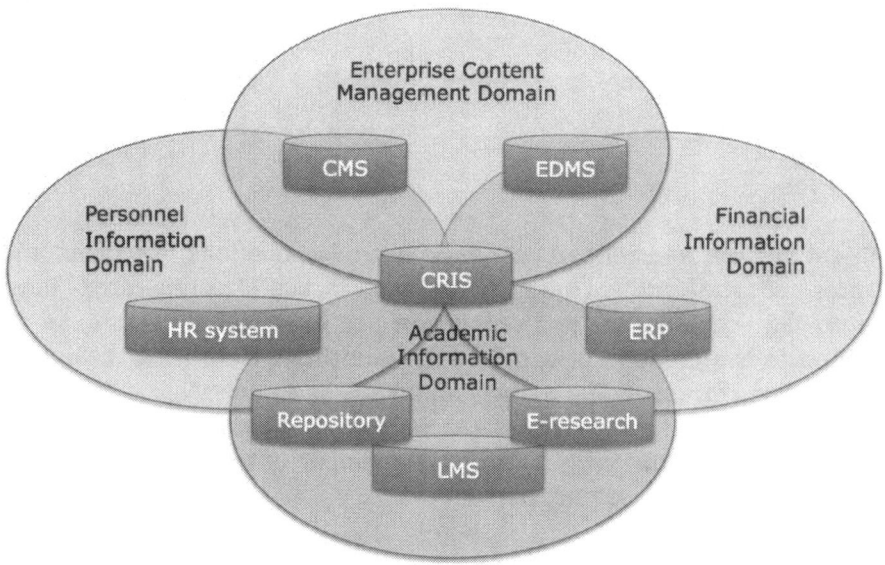

Figure 4. The Enhanced AID model

3.2.1 Introduction to Current Research Information Systems (CRIS)

A CRIS should cover the needs of research management in an increasingly competitive research environment in which research funds are growing and funders require more precise and comprehensive information of the research activities and their output. Therefore, the CRIS should enable research managers and councils easier and better access to measure and analyze research activities more accurately. It also should give researchers easier access to relevant information, for example making project applications easier to complete as the information needed is captured and available when needed, thus eliminating duplicate work. It should also provide data to researchers' personal pages, like CV-pages. It should give entrepreneurs and businesses easy access to new research, thus increasing the diffusion of innovation in the society. It should provide the media and public with easy access to research information.

CRIS's are often based on relational databases but not necessarily: RDF/XML are also used. It is important that semantic relations between research entities can be captured. The typical entities in a CRIS system are the following:

- Person;
- Results (documents, publications, media);
- Organisation;
- Project;
- Event.

All entities are interrelated and have recursive relations. Relations and states of the entities are formalised through enumerated lists, controlled vocabularies, and ontologies. For example, a person can be related to the creation of a publication and have the role of being the author, the corresponding author, an editor, or a supervisor if the publication was a doctoral thesis. If the person is related to a project that person might be the project leader, a member of project staff, a work package leader or a contact person.

It should be clear that data models of CRIS (Based on Razum *et al.*, 2007) are:

- Extensive. Covering several entities, model to cover all or most research activities;
- Detailed. Relations and states are broken down to their most detailed level;
- Formalised. Relations and states are formalised in enumerated lists, and ontologies;
- Logically structured. Often depicted in ER-diagrams.

3.2.2   Common System Features

Existing and current CRIS's are typically interoperable with university systems like Human Resource Management (HRM), LDAP and Content Management Systems (CMS), thus reusing existing and authoritative data in the CRIS and providing exposure of CRIS data in existing information systems. The system has extensive user roles. Examples are the researcher as a personal user, the reporter who can register output from a specific institution, the editor who can reject, accept and edit registrations for one or more departments), the validator who does final validation typically on a supra-organisational level, and the administrator.

Besides being interoperable with the campus information systems, CRIS's usually take advantage of external information providers. This can either be done manually, thus importing data from databases like Web of Science, or by integrating them into the systems as look-ups or 'type-ahead' functions, accessing the data by a web service.

A very important feature is a comprehensive reporting tool. Typically, the systems are primarily conceived with several standard reports. But advanced systems let the user himself create and save reports. Creating and maintaining trustworthy reports is one of the main challenges for CRIS. It requires great care for the metadata in the system. Data must be correct and at a certain stage, data should not be changed anymore or at least there should be a log that provides all information about who did what when. This is why CRIS need an extensive set of roles and advanced workflow.

Most commonly known CRIS systems are listed below. The list is not comprehensive: there are several systems that cover similar tasks apart from the ones mentioned below. However, these are not part of the CRIS community: one example is the German FACTscience used by several faculties of medicine in Germany[44].

Commercial		Open Source / Non Commercial	
Name	URL	Name	URL
PURE	http://www.atira.dk/en/pure/	Metis	http://aptest.uci.kun.nl/metis/service/Metisguide/index.htm Dutch only
UniCRIS	http://www.unicris.com/lenya/uniCRIS/live/index.html	ORBIT	http://orbit.dtu.dk based on http://www.toolxite.dk/metatoo
Converis	http://converis.avedas.com/en /start.html	Lund University Public ations (LUP)	http://lup.lub.lu.se

Table 5. A non-exhaustive list of CRIS systems

---

[44] http://www.factscience.de (last access on November 21st, 2008).

3.2.3 Digital Open Access Repositories

Digital Open Access Repositories are repositories that provide public non-restricted access to content, i.e. full-texts. They are either institutional repositories or discipline-specific. Many of them provide Open Access (OA) only to a sub-set of their content. In this chapter we look to those repositories as Open Access Repositories, common to the DRIVER Guidelines specification[45].

The global Open Access repository community is more concerned with providing access to the full-text than with precision and consistency in the metadata. Metadata is also important, but the primary goal is providing access. Most repositories are representing bibliographic information in the 15 Dublin Core (DC) elements as specified by the OAI-PMH (Lagoze and Van de Sompel, 2001). The low barrier approach has worked very well for the OAI-repositories success, since, at the time of writing, there where around 1250 OAI-compatible repositories worldwide according to OpenDOAR[46]. A disadvantage is that searching in OAI-PMH aggregators, e.g. service provider OAIster, is less than optimal. There has been no international organisation or guidelines specifying what data and how they should be entered in the 15 DC elements. This is one of DRIVER's objectives.

Institutional Repositories are easy to install but hard to master. There are many cases of institutional repositories that are complaining about the difficulties of getting the content in the repositories (Davis and Connolly, 2007). Getting researchers to self-archive is a case of changing culture of a whole research domain so that it becomes prerequisite for researchers in their domain, e.g. astrophysics in Arxiv.org. An alternative approach is simply instructing them to do so. A third solution might be to make it so easy that it is hard not to do it. The last option seems to be possible when there is synergy between repositories and CRIS. As mentioned before, evidence shows that repositories backed by CRIS's seem to be better populated. This observation is supported by the three case studies in this chapter.

---

[45] DRIVER Guidelines: http://www.DRIVER-support.eu/managers.html (last access on November 21st, 2008).

[46] OpenDOAR, Growth of the OpenDOAR database worldwide: http://tinyurl.com/4zs7cg (last access on November 21st, 2008).

Open Access repositories have some important features that are not common in CRIS's:

- Allocation of standard persistent identifiers to uploaded full-texts / objects, i.e. URN, DOI or similar;
- Download statistics to individual objects;
- Usage rights information i.e. machine readable data like Creative Commons licenses.

CRIS and digital OA repositories have overlaps especially with regard to bibliographic metadata and author information.

Commonalities	CRIS and Repositories
Bibliographic metadata	Often more detailed and of better quality in CRIS as a result of imported data from authoritative databases and validation workflows
Author information	Especially internal authors are described in much detail in CRIS systems to ensure correct identification of authors
Vocabularies	Similar vocabularies for publication types exist
Author pages	Data from both CRIS and repository systems are used for personal CV pages for researchers

Table 6. Comparison of CRIS and Repositories

3.2.4 CERIF: the Common European Research Information Format

The CERIF (The Common European Research Information Format) is an international standard for CRIS-interoperability, which according euroCRIS is a data model recommended by the EU to the EU member states[47].

euroCRIS: the Community behind the CERIF Format

The euroCRIS community is a non-for-profit organisation that, according to their website, aims to be the internationally recognised point of reference for all matters relating to CRIS. euroCRIS organises biannual membership meetings, annual seminars and biennial conferences. The organisation also gathers experts within the domain, thus organizing task groups for relevant problems to be discussed and

---

[47] euroCRIS web site: http://www.eurocris.org/public/about-eurocris (last access on November 21st, 2008).

solved; one of them will be mentioned in the next paragraph. Last but not least, euroCRIS is the community behind the CERIF-format today.

euroCRIS has shown an increasing interest in publications as a research result and in digital Open Access repositories. One of the latest indicators of this tendency was the establishment of the CERIF Task Group for Institutional Repositories (IR-CERIF). The task group had its initial meeting at the CRIS2008 conference in Maribor, Slovenia[48]. According to the draft mission statement the task group aims *"To further the science and technology of the linkage between CRIS and repositories and specifically open access institutional repositories of publications [...][49]"*.

When looking at the developments of the CERIF data model, it also becomes clear that publications have become increasingly important in the data model.

History and current Status

The original CERIF format from 1991 only dealt with research projects records. It was recommended to the EU member states as leverage to the exchange of research project data[50]. However, working with CERIF91, it became clear that there was a need to extend to other types of research information. This resulted in CERIF2000 that introduced a full CRIS data model including results from projects e.g. publications, patents, products and organisations, persons, expertises and equipment and facilities. In the 2004 release of CERIF (CERIF2004)[51] the model included three 1st level (core) entities, the Organisation Unit (OrgUnit), Person and Project. Relations between these three entities were made in Dublin Core, thus taking into account the requirements of the Grey Literature community and the increasing number of Open Access repositories based on OAI-PMH and DC (Jeffery, 2000).

In the release of the CERIF format, CERIF2006, released October 2007, publications (ResultPublication) have been 'upgraded' to one of the four Core Entities in the CERIF Data Model.

---

[48] euroCRIS Newsflash, issue 23, June 2008.

[49] euroCRIS Newsflash, issue 22, April 2008.

[50] http://cordis.europa.eu/cerif/src/about.htm#1 (last access on November 21st, 2008).

[51] http://www.dfki.de/~brigitte/CERIF/CERIF2004_1.1FDM/CERIF_FullDataModel_Release1_1_HTML.html (last access on November 21st, 2008).

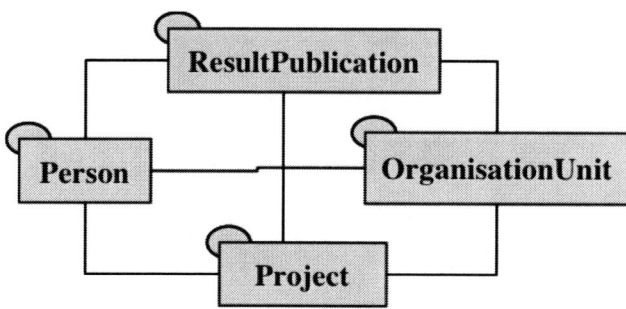

Figure 5. CERIF Core entities (CERIF 2006- 1.1 Full Data model (FDM))[52]

On a second level there are entities that include Event, Products, Patents, Skills, CV, Equipment, Facility, Funding Programme, Service. In comparison to CERIF2004 two major changes have occurred. Firstly the model has been made more scalable, flexible and simple by model normalisation. But most important is the introduction of the so-called semantic layer, containing the classification of entities. This semantic layer has simplified the model by moving all role and type definitions away from each entity to the more generic semantic layer. Last and especially interesting for data exchange was the introduction of the CERIF2006XML Data exchange format specification.

The core and second level entities are connected by the CERIF linking entities (Figure 6). The roles of these linking entities are given by the semantic layer, i.e. Person 'is author of' ResultPublication. Other roles can be given. The semantic layer model allows for capture of any kind of schema or structure. In the table only core entities are connected but core entities can also be connected to 2nd level entities, i.e. ResultPublication 'is funded by' FundingProgramme.

At the moment of this writing, the CERIF2008[53] release was in review. This release is especially interesting for Institutional Repositories and Open Access, as it aims specifically to increase CRIS connectivity to repositories and to elaborate the existing publication model in CERIF2006.

---

[52] See Jörg *et al.*, 2007.

[53] http://www.eurocris.org/cerif/cerif-releases/cerif-2008 (last access on November 21st, 2008).

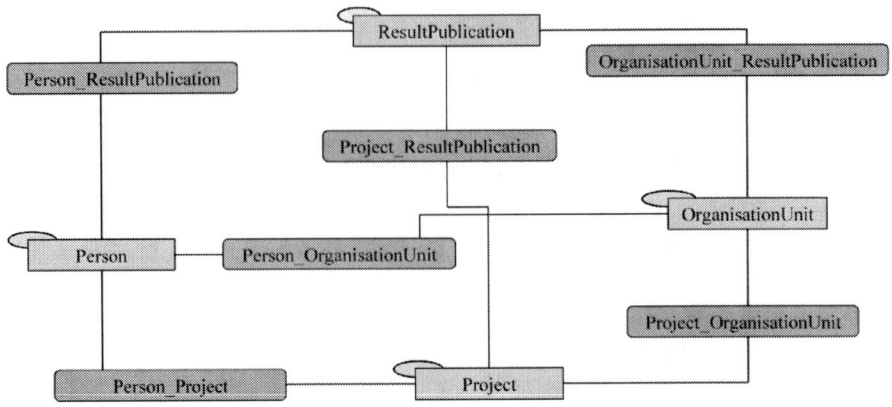

Figure 6. CERIF Link Entities connecting Core Entities

The release does not change the core model structure besides the major extensions to the Publication entity and the Person (PersonName) entity. The task group behind CERIF2008 is lead by Brigitte Jörg (German Research Center for Artificial Intelligence, DFKI, Language Technology Lab). It also includes developers from Atira A/S, the company behind PURE, the commercial CRIS/Digital Repository system that is widely used by universities in Denmark, and has taken in advice from a wider user group of people in the Research Management Community, and also from the University Library and Digital Library community. The elaboration is evident when comparing the publication model from CERIF2006 and CERIF2008 side-by-side (Figures 8a and 8b).

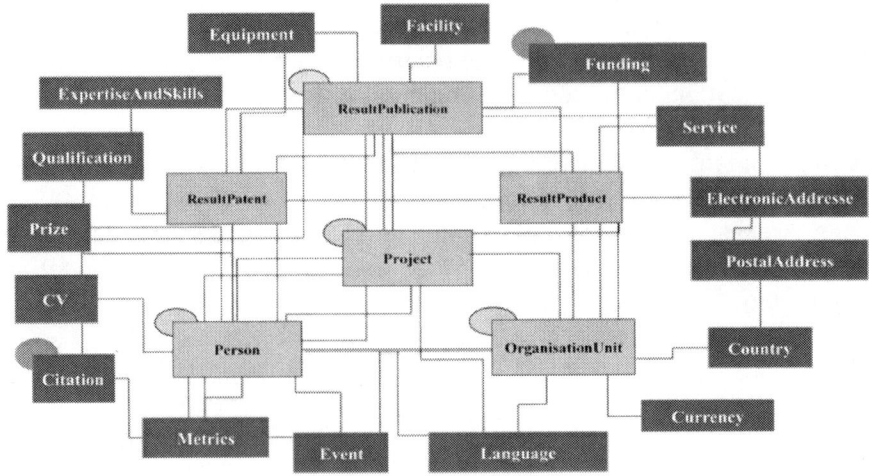

Figure 7. Some CERIF entities and their relationships (CERIF2008)

Relevant for the DRIVER Guidelines, is the extension of the semantic layer for publications that allow for complex classification of publications. The list of publication types is a result of the collaboration of different information domains in the euroCRIS community, in which research management people, system architects and librarians have worked together[54].

cfPublicationTypes

Book	Journal Article Review
Book Review	Conference Proceedings
Book Chapter Abstract	Conference Proceedings Article
Book Chapter Review	Letter
Inbook	Letter to Editor
Anthology	PhD Thesis
Monograph	Doctoral Thesis
Reference book	Report
Textbook	Short communication
Encyclopedia	Poster
Manual	Presentation
Otherbook	Newsclipping
Journal	Commentary
Journal Article	Annotation
Journal Article Abstract	

3.2.5 Bringing the two Information Domains together

One important task for DRIVER-CRIS interoperability is to help prevent institutional and international silo effects. The repository community has worked on making repositories interoperable through the OAI-PMH model. It cannot be denied that the low barrier strategy has realised a large uptake in the library and research community, although it has been criticised for its use of unqualified Dublin Core and all the problems that have resulted from bad quality metadata. Organisational uptake proves to be at least as important as technical interoperability. Several industry cases show that it is not always the best product that wins the market, e.g. VHS/Betamax. Critical mass is essential for interoperability. It is not very useful to implement the most open and state-of-the-art research management system if you are the only one using it. DRIVER-CRIS interoperability might have the synergy that provides the leverage for the spreading of CRIS and the metadata quality for digital repositories.

---

[54] The CERIF2008 semantic layer (Jörg *et al.*, 2008).

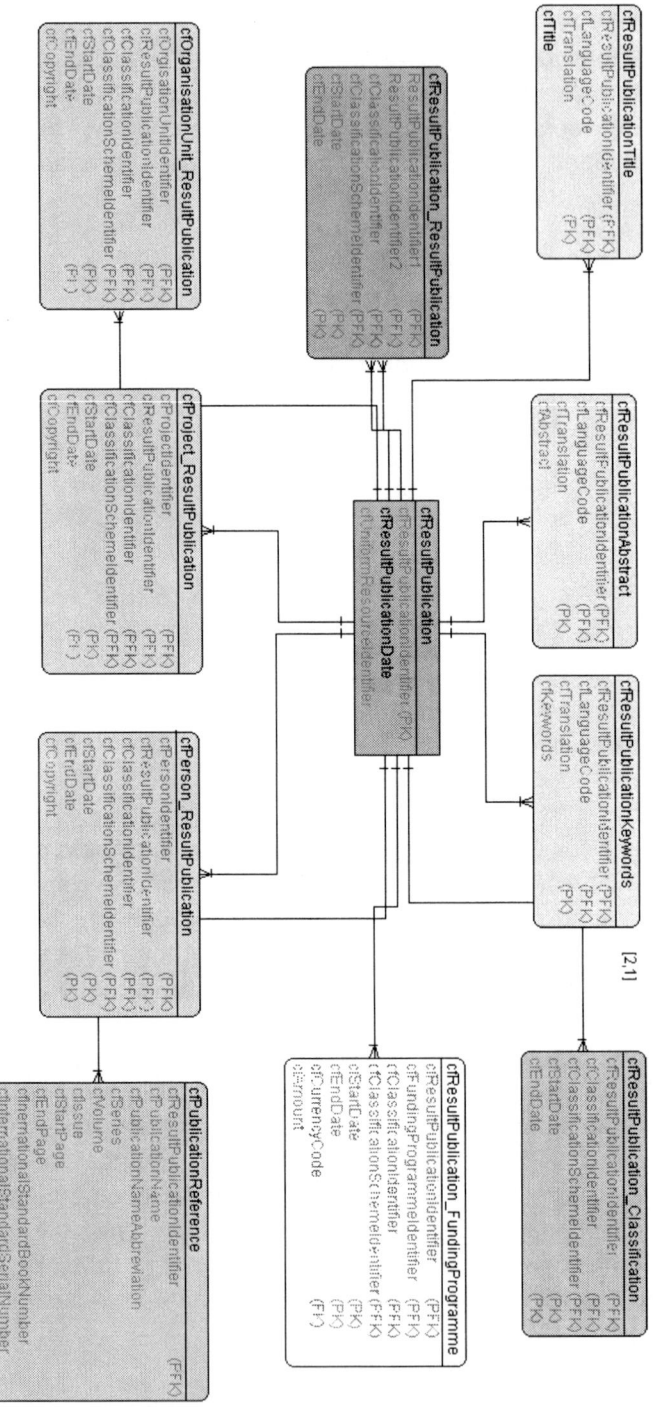

Figure 8a. CERIF2006 Core Entity Result Publication

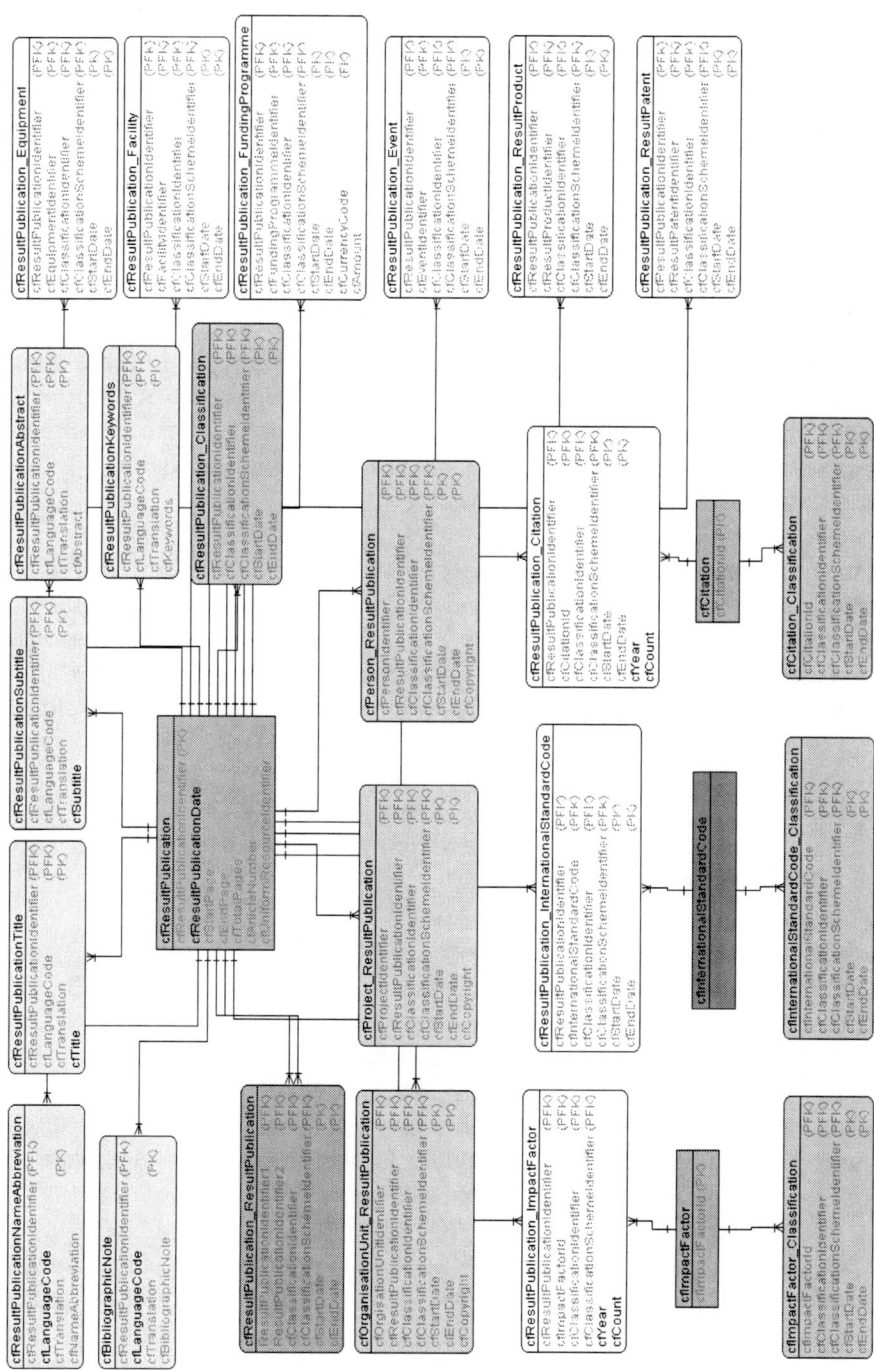

Figure 8b. CERIF2008 Core entity ResultPublication

59

Another important element is that the two systems are addressing academics. Hence, securing interoperability between CRIS and digital repositories will prevent the so-called keystroke problem or the problem with double entries. The Irish case study illustrates the positive impact of having a university wide information system policy that focuses on the researcher and requires interoperable information systems by eliminating all double entries.

Because a joint European infrastructure for CRIS systems has been pushed by the ESF-Eurohorcs report *Window to Science* (ESF, 2008:10), it seems that repositories and CRIS systems are both aiming for a one-stop access point to a joint infrastructure, one of the many things they have in common. It would be beneficial for both communities to collaborate further by building a common European e-Infrastructure for research.

Finally, the KE Institutional Repositories Workshop Exchanging Research Information concluded *"that achieving interoperability between CRIS and digital repositories is desirable and would not only benefit research administrators and librarians as maintainers of these systems, but would create an added value to researchers as well, at least avoiding double input of data."*

3.3 Case Studies in Ireland, Denmark and The Netherlands

3.3.1 Ireland, Trinity College Dublin Repository
Universities in Ireland have successfully integrated their CRIS and Institutional Repositories. They have also made it attractive for researchers to self-archive in the repositories. In this case study, the reason why Ireland and especially Trinity College Dublin (TCD) have succeeded with their CRIS/Institutional Repository integration, will be investigated. Then, the future plans for Expertise Ireland and its role as host for the national research portal will follow.

TCD's CRIS is called the Research Support System or RSS. It is based on the CERIF2002 data model. RSS collects information about employees at TCD directly from the Human Resources system. CV and publication data are added as specified in the CERIF2002 use of Dublin Core metadata. Bibliographic metadata are added by importing data from external sources like ISI and manual input. Data are exposed to external portals, in particular Expertiseireland.com, through a web service. Internally at TCD, data from RSS are shared with the Institutional Repository through a web service. The data are synchronised so that changes in a record in any of the two systems are reflected in both systems, thus excluding any anomalies between the two. Bibliographic data between the two are exchanged in qualified Dublin Core.

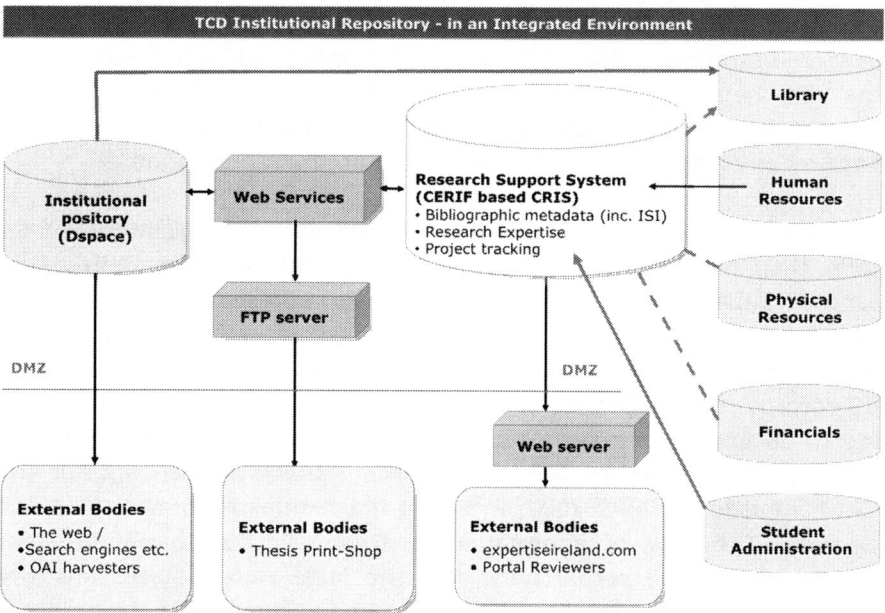

Figure 9. An integrated view on information systems at TCD

Researchers Curriculum Vitae as driver

According to Niamh Brennan, Programme Manager of Research Information Systems & Services at TCD, one very important reason for their success is a strong focus from the very beginning on the researchers as users. The first implementation of CRIS started in 2001, the system still being an in-house development based on Oracle, as there was no on-the-shelf system that provided the required features.

> "A coherent information policy for College to address the needs of management, the Library, e-learning, electronic publications and records management will be developed with a view to having an integrated view of information systems across the whole of College." (TCD strategic plan)

Brennan explains that an important aspect of the successful implementation process of the CRIS is that it is driven by Curriculum Vitae (CV). One of the reasons for letting the web CV's become the driver of the CRIS implementation was that this was one of the main concerns of the academics. As there are no researcher evaluation or mandates 'forcing' the academics to use the CRIS, the only approach for a successful implementation was to know what motivates the researchers, thus using web CV's , being an appealing feature in 2001, as a carrot. Moreover, the strategy of the TCD information policy has been focused from the very beginning on having an integrated view of information systems. It is important that no information should be entered more than once by any researcher in the university information systems.

For most researchers publications are the most important items in their CV's, their projects coming second. Researchers are repeatedly asked for their publication lists, e.g. when applying for research funds. In case of the research database of TCD, full integration with complementary systems is catered for. HR-systems ensure automated pre-population of CV-records. Once updated in the CRIS, the information is automatically fed to all appropriate systems, personal web pages, university pages, all external to Expertise Ireland. The interoperability is ensured as the CRIS is based on CERIF2002, including the entities for publications and persons. The flow of information from one source to all-important showcases for the researchers, like the local web systems and the national expert portal Expertise Ireland, ensures that researchers experience that their efforts in updating their profiles are worthwhile.

The Institutional Repository
The process of implementing the CRIS has taught TCD a lot about the motivations of the researchers when it comes to the implementation of IT-systems that interfere with the academics' workflow. When TCD wanted to implement their DSpace Institutional Repository in 2005, it was obvious that the system would be integrated as much as possible with the existing information systems. Thus integration with the existing CRIS system was essential to avoid double entry of data. For the integration of CRIS and the Institutional Repository, TCD took advantage of qualified DUBLIN CORE-metadata in DSpace and the DUBLIN CORE publication data in CERIF2002. The researcher has little interaction with the actual Institutional Repository. Publication data are pulled in from various resources such as Scopus, ISI Thomson Scientific and in many cases all that the researcher needs to do is to upload the full-text. In the Research Support System (CRIS), the researcher sees

an overview of publications that matches the researcher as author and he can claim records as his own publications.

To claim an article, place a tick in the check box beside it and press the save button.
To unclaim an article remove the tick from the check box and press the save button

Claim	Author	Article Number	Article Title	Journal
☐	ROBERTSON, AHF	46342389	THE GEOLOGICAL HISTORY OF MAIO, CAPE VERDE ISLANDS	J GEOL SOC LONDON
☐	ROBERTSON, AHF	45491924	THE MESOZOIC AND TERTIARY HISTORY OF MAIO, CAPE VERDE ISLANDS	J GEOL SOC LONDON
☐	ROBERTSON, I	20876966	"BUSY DOING NOTHING?" INCREASED RIGHT FRONTAL AND PARIETAL ACTIVATION ASSOCIATED WITH SELF-SUSTAINED ATTENTION TO AN 'UNCHALLENGING' TASK	NEUROIMAGE
☐	ROBERTSON, I	114541238	AN ELECTROPHYSIOLOGICAL PREDICTOR OF IMMINENT ACTION ERROR IN HUMANS	J COGNITIVE NEUROSCI
☐	ROBERTSON, I	112981740	THE EVALUATION AND TREATMENT OF MILD TRAUMATIC BRAIN INJURY	NEUROPSYCHOLOGIA
☐	ROBERTSON, IH	24152919	BRIEF MINDFULNESS TRAINING FOR ATTENTIONAL PROBLEMS AFTER TRAUMATIC BRAIN INJURY: A RANDOMISED CONTROL TREATMENT TRIAL	NEUROPSYCHOL REHABIL
☐	ROBERTSON, IH	126555502	COGNITIVE NEUROSCIENCE AND BRAIN REHABILITATION: A PROMISE KEPT	J NEUROL NEUROSUR PS
☐	ROBERTSON, IH	114333673	COGNITIVE REHABILITATION IN CLINICAL NEUROPSYCHOLOGY	BRAIN COGNITION
☐	ROBERTSON, IH	111992966	COGNITIVE REHABILITATION ATTENTION AND NEGLECT	TRENDS COGN SCI
☐	ROBERTSON, IH	114877651	COMPENSATIONS FOR BRAIN DEFICITS. "EVERY CLOUD…"	BRIT J PSYCHIAT
☐	ROBERTSON, IH	120486623	DO WE NEED THE "LATERAL" IN UNILATERAL NEGLECT? SPATIALLY NONSELECTIVE ATTENTION DEFICITS IN UNILATERAL NEGLECT AND THEIR IMPLICATIONS FOR REHABILITATION	NEUROIMAGE
☐	ROBERTSON, IH	114789966	IMPROVING THE CLINICAL DIAGNOSIS OF PERSONAL NEGLECT: A REFORMULATED COMB AND RAZOR TEST	CORTEX
☐	ROBERTSON, IH	121349080	INTERACTION OF HAND USE AND SPATIAL SELECTIVE ATTENTION IN CHILDREN	NEUROPSYCHOLOGIA
☐	ROBERTSON, IH	122307305	REHABILITATION OF ATTENTION: BOTH AN END AND A MEANS TO AN END	BRAIN COGNITION
☐	ROBERTSON, IH	111615136	REHABILITATION OF BRAIN DAMAGE: BRAIN PLASTICITY AND PRINCIPLES OF GUIDED RECOVERY	PSYCHOL BULL
☐	ROBERTSON, IH	122958521	REHABILITATION OF EXECUTIVE FUNCTION: FACILITATION OF EFFECTIVE GOAL MANAGEMENT ON COMPLEX TASKS USING PERIODIC AUDITORY ALERTS	NEUROPSYCHOLOGIA
☐	ROBERTSON, IH	114553688	REHABILITATION OF EXECUTIVE FUNCTIONING: AN EXPERIMENTAL-CLINICAL VALIDATION OF GOAL MANAGEMENT TRAINING	J INT NEUROPSYCH SOC
☐	ROBERTSON, IH	119303869	SETTING GOALS FOR COGNITIVE REHABILITATION	CURR OPIN NEUROL
☐	ROBERTSON, IH	123316859	THE DIFFERENTIAL ASSESSMENT OF CHILDREN'S ATTENTION: THE TEST OF EVERYDAY ATTENTION FOR CHILDREN (TEA-CH). NORMATIVE SAMPLE AND ADHD PERFORMANCE	J CHILD PSYCHOL PSYC

Figure 10. The researchers' overview of publications that have been imported to RSS

63

Claiming a publication pre-fills the metadata for the record, limiting the effort needed for entering bibliographic data.

Afterwards, the author can share the record with colleagues, e.g. co-authors, and then upload the full-text. Finally, the record is reviewed and archived by the library staff. In the review process, the staff checks the version of the full-text with the Sherpa/ROMEo service and contacts the researcher directly by phone if there are any issues with the version. Brennan explains that this personal contact also helps them to identify early adaptors and Open Access enthusiasts. A big advantage of this design is that the researcher does not have to bother with a new system, but naturally maintains and updates his CV in a system that he has already accepted and that is integrated in the information flow at TCD.

National Institutional Repository development in Ireland

From 2007 onwards, the Irish universities have been granted a three year project[55] to build Open Access repositories in each Irish university and develop a federated harvesting and discovery service via a national portal. The project is directed by the Irish Universities Association (IUA) and managed by the IUA librarians' group. The portal is to be hosted by Expertise Ireland that will provide a single point of access to Irish research output. IREL-Open project will provide the Institutional Repository infrastructure as a part of the Irish National Research Platform Infrastructure. The idea is that the portal will provide access to Expertise Ireland, Institutional Repositories, research data, 4th Level Ireland and the Researcher Mobility Portal. The objective of the single point for research information access is to:

- Highlight the extent and quality of Ireland's research effort, and to attract the best researchers to Ireland;
- Promote the expertise, capabilities and innovation of the higher education and public research sector;
- Provide a platform to increase collaboration between industry and academia and in particular to allow development agency staff to facilitate such collaboration in key strategic areas;
- Promote networking to make it easier for academics to set up interdisciplinary, inter-institutional and international research;

---

[55] The IREL-Open project: http://www.irel-open.ie (last access on November 21st, 2008).

- Explore and develop collaborative or contract opportunities that are of interest to industry and that may draw industry investment (direct or indirect);
- Provide Assessment/Benchmarking of research output to stakeholders;
- Provide a platform for industry users to address specific research and innovation needs;
- Promote the technology offers from the higher education and public research system and enhance the take up of licensing opportunities;
- Attract post graduate students to double the number of PhD students;
- Increase the base of information on the national research effort available to IDA Ireland executives in their marketing of Ireland for high tech foreign direct investment;
- Generate bi-lateral agreement between the research entity and the companies that generate research activities, develop technologies or design products.

TCD is also making an effort to map CERIF DC data into the DRIVER Guidelines Dublin Core. Brennan concludes that other institutions in Ireland are seeing the benefits of the model employed at TCD.

3.3.2 The Netherlands, national NARCIS Portal

Current Research Information Systems are well integrated in the Dutch Universities. All universities have implemented and are using the CRIS system METIS. KNAW (Royal Netherlands Academy of Art and Sciences) also has significant experience with collecting data from distributed heterogeneous academic information systems in the national research portal NARCIS. The research portal collects data from institutional repositories, CRIS's and e-data from the EASY. In this case study we will take a closer look at the widely used METIS CRIS system and how it interacts with the institutional repositories. But first we will investigate the infrastructure of the research portal NARCIS.

Joining three Information Domains in NARCIS

NARCIS[56] is the first step towards creating a one-stop-shop to Dutch Academic Information. According to the website NARCIS provides access to 249,579 scientific publications, of which 185,375 in Open

---

[56] National Academic Research and Collaborations Information System - NARCIS http://www.narcis.info *(last access on December 10th, 2008).*

Access, and 6,600 data sets, and information on researchers (expertise), research projects and research institutes in the Netherlands[57].

The portal is an attempt to collect and expose information from three different information domains NOD, DAREnet and EASY. NOD is the national aggregation of the CRIS data, DAREnet is the national service provider for institutional repositories providing Open Access to publicly-funded Dutch research and EASY collects and exposes a large number of research datasets (Baars *et al.*, 2008). NARCIS could be called the Academic Information Domain in which all three sub-information domains are aggregated (Razum *et al.*, 2007).

NOD[58] is the national aggregation of CRIS data that provides public access to information of current research programmes and research projects, researchers and their expertises and affiliation, and profiles of research institutions. Data in NOD are highly structured and kept in a relational database. Most of the data are aggregated from the 14 local METIS implementations at universities and research institutions in the Netherlands. However, it is also possible to register data directly into NOD in case the institution does not have a CRIS.

DAREnet[59] (Digital Academic Repositories) was launched in January 2004 as a first network of its kind providing uniform access to all Open Access repositories in The Netherlands. DAREnet had two subsets, Cream of Science and Promise of Science[60]. Especially the Cream of Science project attracted a lot of attention when it was launched in May 2005, providing Open Access to approximately 60% of all publications from more than 200 top researchers (Feijen and van der Kuil, 2005). The four-year DARE programme was concluded in late 2006 and KNAW took over the ownership of DAREnet. DAREnet continued as an independent service provider to Open Access repositories in The Netherlands until June 2008. Today it is an integrated part of the national science portal NARCIS.

---

[57] As accessed on September 24th, 2009.

[58] http://www.onderzoekinformatie.nl/en/oi (last access on November 21st, 2008).

[59] http://www.surffoundation.nl/smartsite.dws?ch=ENG&id=13778 (last access on November 21st, 2008).

[60] http://www.narcis.info/?wicket:interface=:7:::: and
http://www.narcis.info/?wicket:interface=:8:::: (last access on November 21st, 2008).

Nederlands

narcis

The gateway to Dutch scientific information

NARCIS provides access to 249,579 scientific publications (185,375 of which are open access publications), 6,600 data sets, and information on researchers (expertise), research projects and research institutes in the Netherlands.

narcis
Home

[   ] (search)

☑ Organisations ☑ Persons ☑ Current research ☑ Data sets ☑ Publications [all publications ▼]

Scientific news from other sources (Dutch)

Repressie in Iran laait op (ScienceGuide, 24-09-2009)
Het academisch jaar is in Iran gisteren geopend. De machthebbers hebben studenten gevangen gezet en de toegang tot studies geweigerd ter voorkoming van herleefd protest.

Utrechts hbo en wo op agenda VN (ScienceGuide, 24-09-2009)
Tijdens een werkbezoek van de UNCTAD aan Utrecht hebben de HKU en de UU met succes aandacht gevraagd voor hun onderzoek, onderwijs en ondernemerschap in de creatieve economie.

Een brutaal schaap heeft succes, maar sterft jong (NRC Handelsblad | Wetenschap, 24-09-2009)
Brutale mannetjesschapen planten zich snel voort, maar sterven ook snel. De geduldige rammen trekken aan het langste eind.

more scientific news (Dutch)

Research Institutes

- Delft University of Technology
- Erasmus University Rotterdam
- Leiden University
- Maastricht University
- Netherlands Organization for Scientific Research
- Nyenrode Business University

- Open University of the Netherlands
- Radboud University Nijmegen
- Royal Netherlands Academy of Arts and Sciences - KNAW
- Technische Universiteit Eindhoven
- Tilburg University
- University for Humanistics

- University of Amsterdam
- University of Groningen
- University of Twente
- Utrecht University
- Vrije Universiteit Amsterdam
- Wageningen University and Research Centre

repositories | about NARCIS | contact

🏛 KNAW

© 2006-2009 KNAW

Figure 11. The front page of the NARCIS portal

EASY (Electronic Archiving System)[61] provides an infrastructure for collection, depositing and accessing datasets. The system is maintained by DANS (Data Archiving and Networked Services). Data are deposited by researchers or data managers directly into the central web based EASY interface. Most of the content in EASY is Open Access, while some of the data requires the user to contact the owner of the data to ask permission.

The three information domains are distinct from each other, having different origins, life cycles and target groups. Information in CRIS's is typically managed by administrators and interoperable with local infor-mation systems at universities, OARs typically by librarians, and data sets by data managers. Collectively, they make for an Academic Information Domain. Thus researchers are affiliated to institutions where they do research in projects and produce datasets that they publish in articles. NARCIS aims to join these relations in one research portal.

However, joining data from individual and heterogeneous sources is a real challenge. Baars *et al.* (2008) have divided the challenges into organisational and technical aspects. The creation of NARCIS benefited from the Repository Managers working group that have been main-tained, also after the conclusion of the DARE programme. *"It is fair to say that, without good organisational structure and agreements about metadata and technical issues, it is impossible to create an AID on national level"* (Baars *et al.*, 2008: 81). On the technical side, KNAW chose to use OAI-PMH as the protocol for harvesting heterogeneous metadata with one protocol, thus only mapping of the index needed between the different XML schemas. Metadata from repositories are based on DC, DIDL[62], and the wrapper format Metadata Object Description Schema (MODS). As for metadata from NOD are CERIF-based XML only a subset of the fields are harvested and indexed, users can obtain the full record directly from the CRIS.

To make the user experience of the NARCIS research portal homoge-nous, even though data are from different sources, the Digital Author Identification (DAI) has been introduced. The DAI provides a unique and persistent identifier to all authors in the Academic Information

---

[61] http://easy.dans.knaw.nl/dms (last access on November 21st, 2008).
[62] http://en.wikipedia.org/wiki/Digital_Item_Declaration_Language (last access on November 21st, 2008).

Domain, thus enabling the user to find a researcher and with one click identify all publications, activities and e-data from a single researcher (as in Figure 10).

In 2007 SURF started a new programme SURFshare. This programme aims to upgrade the Dutch Repository Infrastructure for Enhanced Publications, based on the OAI-ORE standard. One of the initiatives is the definition of an interoperable Persistent Identifier for Objects (PId).

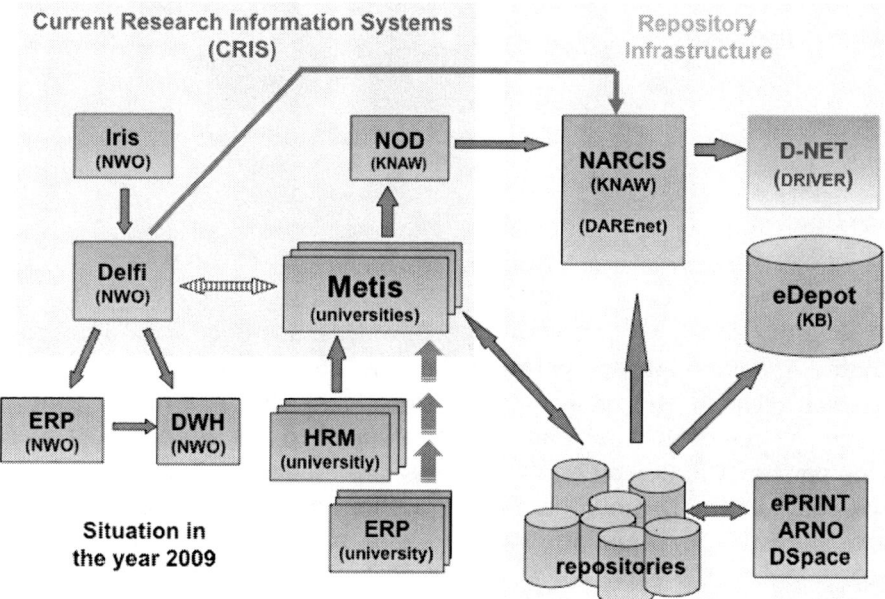

Figure 12. Research Information Landscape of the Netherlands

METIS, the Dutch CRIS Software

METIS is the Dutch CRIS software used to record the activities and results of research in the Netherlands. The system is developed and maintained by the University Centre for Information Services (UCI) at Radboud University Nijmegen. The two people behind the development are Hans Schoonbrood and Eduard J. Simons, who are in charge of the METIS competence centre at UCI and provided very useful input to this description of METIS.

Fourteen Dutch universities are using METIS. It is CERIF-compatible, but designed to suit the particular needs of Dutch universities and as such it does not replicate the official CERIF model as given by the euroCRIS organisation.

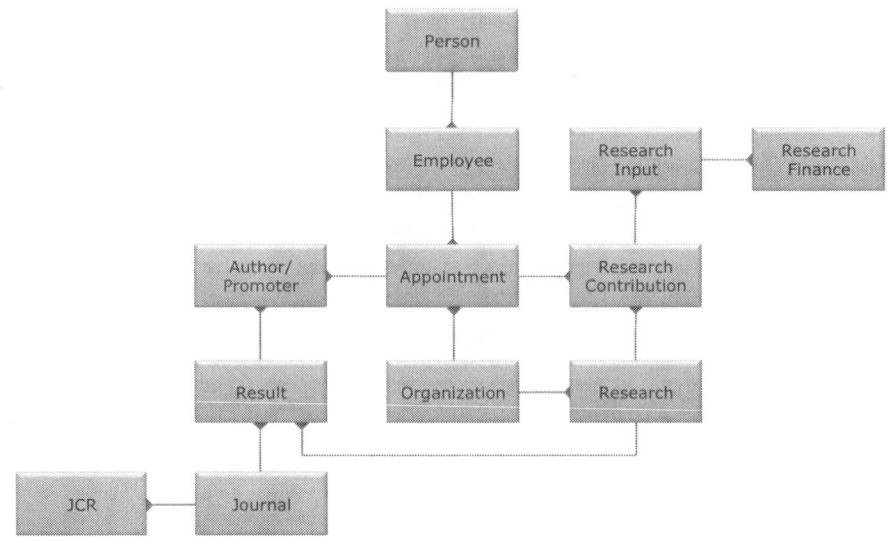

Figure 13. Entity Relationship Diagram (ERD) of METIS

The Entity Relationship Diagram (ERD) of METIS is built around the core entity Appointment. Appointment contains information of a relation of a person (researcher) to a given organisational unit at a given point in time. All research input and output is linked to the appointment(s) of the person. The Person entity contains information that can identify the person, like the DAI number (digital author identification), the Person is an Employee by Appointment. Here are some examples of relations using the METIS ERD: The Person is an Author of a research Result by Appointment to an Organisation. Organisations do Research (like projects). Persons Appointed to an affiliated Organisation contributed to a research (project) with a specific role.

The following table gives an overview of the entities in the METIS data model.

Person	**Employee**
Under this header, the unique information about a researcher is registered, including: birth date, gender, unique METIS ID, DAI num-ber (digital author identification) and the number from the human resource management system, mostly SAP or ORACLE HR.	All names (preferred name, name variants and aliases) are registered under the entity 'employee'. A person can have one or more names. All various names under which a person publishes are registered in METIS.

Organisation

All organisational units relevant for research (faculties, research institutes, expertise centres), including the parent and child relations, e.g. department under faculty. For each organisational unit a vast amount of data is registered, among which the name, address, url, contact person, type of the unit, date of creation and closing-down date of the unit, if applicable.

Research (projects)

Under this header, information concerning the research activity as such is registered: title of the research, description, start and end dates, url, sponsor(s), type of research, methodology, relations to other research, leading unit for the research, progress of the research, various classification schemes including the following thesauri: MESH (Medical subject headings), ISN, NABS, NBC and JEL.

Appointment

Information on the appointment of a researcher at a given organisational unit. This is a core entity in METIS. All research input and output (results) is linked to the appointment of the researcher. The appointment concerns the relation between the employee and the organisational unit, including the function of the researcher and the nature and duration of the appointment. A researcher can have one or more appointments in METIS, at the same time as well as successive appointments.

Author

The researcher in his role as producer of academic output. The authorship can be linked to one or more appointments, and thus organisational units.

Promoter

The person(s) supervising, coaching or judging a PhD, including members of the so-called 'reading commission'.

Results

This entity covers all kinds of output of research. At this moment, the following 19 different types of results are distinguished within METIS, each with its appropriate bibliographical description: annotation; article - letter to the editor; article in volume – proceedings; book - monograph - book editorial; book editorship; book review; contribution weekly - daily journal; doctoral thesis; external report; inaugural speech; internal report; journal editorship – referee; lecture; newspaper article; other output; part of book – chapter; patent; recognition; and scientific positions.

Journal

The information about journals in METIS not only covers the name and the ISSN number, but also possible alternative names like abbreviated name, sci name, date of creation and discontinuation of the journal and the copyright notice, if applicable. Some of the publishers, the so-called green publishers, allow the publication of full-text articles from their journals into repositories, if certain conditions are fulfilled.

Impact factor (JCR)

Under this header, the JCR (Journal Citation Report) impact information is registered, i.e. the impact factor of the journals in a given year and for a given discipline, whether the journal is a "top-10" journal and to which quartile it belongs.

Research contribution

Researchers contribute time and capacity to a research from a given appointment. These contributions have certain duration and a researcher can contribute at the same time or consecutively to various research activities, such as projects and programmes. The information on the contribution also includes the 'role' of the researcher in the research activity: head of research, tutor, contact, coach, researcher, PhD, referent, initiator and so on.

Research input (FTE)

The contribution of a given researcher to research expressed in terms of full time equivalents. Furthermore it is possible in METIS to distinguish this input according to 'funding type', i.e. the financing source. There are three types: the government (1st funding), the national research agency (2nd), and commercial companies (3rd). For each of these funding types it is possible to make a distinction between planned and actually realised input.

Research finance

Detailed information on the research financing bodies.

Classification schemas & thesauri

See above under "research".

Table 7. METIS entities

METIS Interfaces

Similar to the CRIS systems in Ireland and Denmark, METIS interfaces with the HRM-system reuse data already registered in the HRM-system of the university. METIS also interfaces with the institutional repositories. It is possible to upload a full-text from METIS directly to a repository. A web service then returns the attributed URL to the full-text in the repository. The bibliographic metadata registered in METIS is transferred to the repository. Moreover, METIS provides an important feature that allows importing bibliographic information from various external sources, including RIS, Bibtex, Web of Science, and Medline.

The user-interfaces of METIS are separated in four different tasks target groups:

- *Public*
  1. Consult METIS, the public search interface that allows users to search the content of the CRIS.

- *Restricted to authorised users*
  2. Data entry and control functions, specifically Administrative registering and updating Results, Contributions, Research and management of the database;
  3. Management Information Module. Module specially designed for research administrators providing assessment data;
  4. Personal METIS, the authors/researchers access to registering and keeping control of own research output. Imported data that is matching an author is also shown here.

Concluding on the Dutch Model of the Academic Information Domain

KNAW and SURF put a lot of effort into bringing the Academic Information Domain together in the national research portal NARCIS. Especially the inclusion of e-data with CRIS and data from repositories, 'glued' together with Digital Author ID, seems very promising. The lessons that are learned in the Netherlands will most likely define the repository infrastructures in other European countries in the years to come, as it has been the case before with DAREnet. NARCIS already provides data to the DRIVER infrastructure, thus participating in the development of DRIVER towards CRIS interoperability. From ultimo 2009 the National Research Database will act as a Dutch hub for delivering data to D-Net of DRIVER. This infrastructure will ensure that the development of metadata formats in The Netherlands are aligned making the alignment to DRIVER a non-issue for the local repository managers.

3.3.3 Denmark, integrated CRIS-OAR Systems

Denmark has a long tradition of collecting and presenting information about research output in a central research portal. The latest version of the Danish National Research Database provides access to almost 500.000 scholarly records, an increasing number of these include Open Access to full-text. Danish universities have succeeded in implementing repositories that combine CRIS and IR capabilities. In this case study, the integration of digital repositories and CRIS systems has provided positive synergies at different levels from individual researchers, to universities, the research portal and finally at central governmental level.

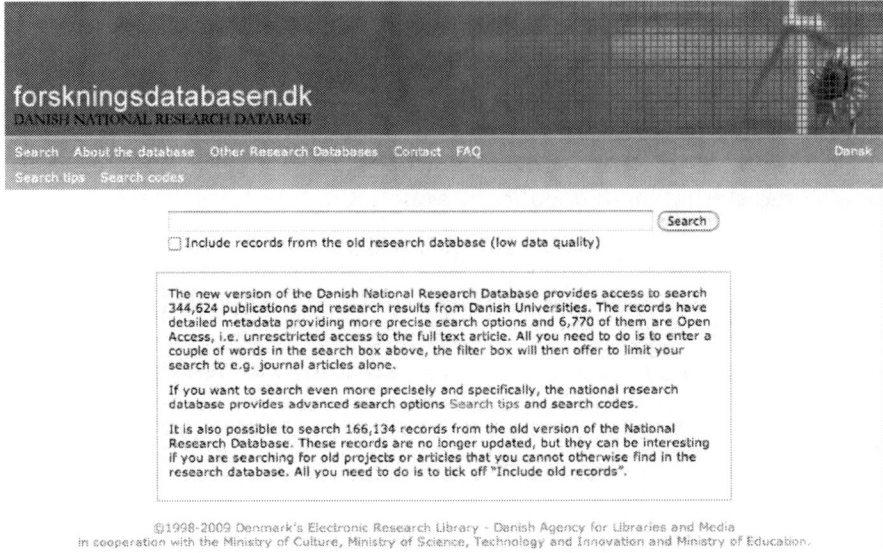

Figure 14. Screenshot from the National Danish research Database

A short History of the Danish Model for Research Registration

The first National Danish Research Database was introduced in the late eighties of the 20th Century. It was a central database where Danish universities and research institutions could provide data about projects, publications, organisations and researchers. The data were put in the database either by batch uploads from local data providers or by registering data directly into a central registration interface. However, these two forms of providing data lacked data quality, timeliness and correctness of data. Moreover, as a central database, the National Research Database was detached from the local institutions and their local databases, and, as a consequence, the data providers lost the ownership and responsibility for their own records. This led to an increasing number of incorrect and out-dated records and a growing need for human intervention in updating and validating the data, a Sisyphean task.

In the late nineties there was growing interest in communicating research activities to the institutions and society (Price, 2008). This led more universities to develop their own systems or adapt existing systems for the collection, storage and exposure of research output. At

74

many universities, university libraries that had already registered publications from their universities in their library catalogues took up this task, considering it to be a natural expansion of their service.

From the year 2000 on, a parallel development took place at Aalborg University (AAU) and Technical University of Denmark (DTU). They started to develop integrated systems that could collect, preserve and expose data about research, publications, projects, persons/experts, activities/events, organisations and thus function as institutional repositories. These systems could also ensure the quality of the collected data, having built-in workflows for validation and quality control. Below is an example of the flexible and customizable workflow in Orbit. The users can decide to have one, two or three levels of validation workflow. A typical workflow is number three from above, where the researcher registers a publication and the department proof-reader validates that the record was indeed a publication of the researcher, and finally the record is validated centrally to ensure metadata quality. This is typically done by a librarian.

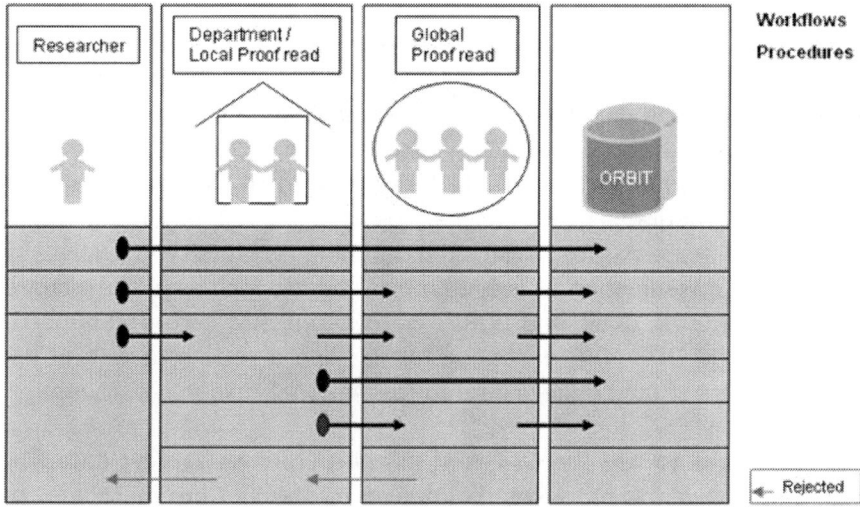

Figure 15. Orbit registration and validation workflow

Finally, the new systems provide a portal and structured data is exposed as web services for use by local department websites and OAI-PMH for external data exchange.

The development of DTU's research database Orbit was closely affiliated to the university library[63]. Similarly, at AAU, the library worked together with a small Internet development company to develop VBN (Knowledge Database Northern Jutland). The company later became known as Atira A/S. Today it develops PURE and markets it as a modular Current Research Information System and Institutional Repository[64]. Both systems use existing data from i.e. the Universities HR-systems through open APIs in a SOA-like manner.

In 2005, DEFF[65]supported the implementation of PURE at four other Danish universities. The collaboration matured the PURE-application and more institutions have followed. Today, all but one university in Denmark have implemented PURE, and the Technical University of Denmark has its own CRIS/OAR system, Orbit. With the introduction of these central university repositories with decentralised institution-wide registration of data, finally there was an infrastructure of repositories embedded in local institutions. With standardised metadata that could be harvested to a central service provider, it became possible to search in a large proportion of the Danish research production.

DDF-MXD, a common exchange Format for Research Publications
In 2004–2005, the development of a new exchange format for research metadata was financed by DEFF, Denmark. It entailed an analysis of the former internal format of the National Danish Research Database and the international CERIF format, as well as the emerging Danish Institutional Repositories. Also, the ongoing university initiatives to standardise classification of research documents, including the research database systems Orbit and PURE, were taken into consideration. The result was the DDF-MXD exchange format and a reconstruction of how data providers should deliver data to the national research database.

The vision was to use the OAI-PMH infrastructure to harvest data from local data providers, but instead of delivering Dublin Core metadata, the DDF-MXD exchange format was developed as a data format with a

---

[63] http://orbit.dtu.dk (last access on November 21st, 2008).

[64] http://atira.dk/en/pure (last access on November 21st, 2008).

[65] Denmark's electronic research library (DEFF):
http://www.deff.dk/default.aspx?lang=english (last access on November 21st, 2008).

richer vocabulary and structured XML data that could secure better automatic validation and richer data for better search facilities.

The first release of the exchange format is called MXD (Metadata Exchange Format for Documents) thus indicating that the format is aimed at handling metadata describing documents. *"As DDF-MXD only serves to describe documents* [one of the five DDF information objects in Figure 16] *it has a simple architecture with a few elements describing the document itself and four elements describing the relations to the four other information objects of the model."* (DDF-MXD 1.2.0: 5)[66].

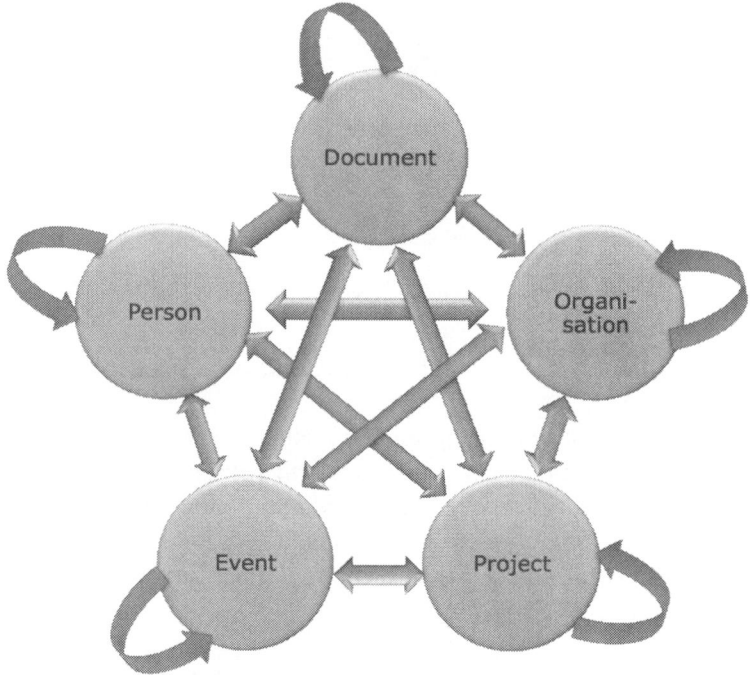

Figure 16. The general DDF exchange model

At present, the only DDF information object that has been developed and released is the MXD. An exchange format for projects is planned for development in the autumn of 2008, in cooperation of Technical Information Centre of Denmark, the Faculty of Life Science at the University of Copenhagen and DEFF.

---

[66] http://www.forskningsdatabasen.dk/About.html (last access on November 21st, 2008).

DDF-MXD is organised in eight main elements.

- Four elements that describe the actual document: Title; Description; Publication information; and Local information.
- Four surrounding elements, representing elements related to the document: Person; Organisation; Project; and Event.

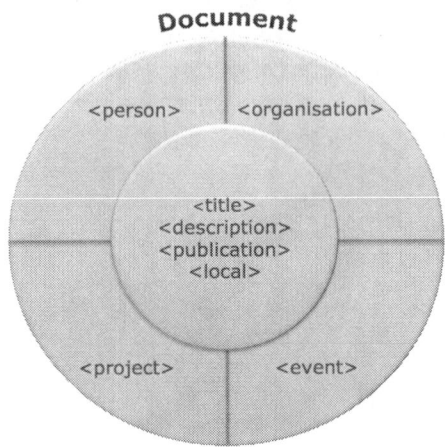

Figure 17. Organisation of the DDF-MXD format

The first four elements in the middle of the model are elements that describe a document:

- Title of the document and an optional translated title;
- Description, includes abstract, keywords and subject classification;
- Publication, contains all the information about how the document was published, including electronic availability;
- Local, contains additional local information that may be formatted to local preferences.

The last four elements in the DDF-MXD format are only described minimally so that the most crucial information about related events, organisations, persons and projects is in the metadata of the document. Each element has an identifier that enables connecting the related information objects. However, as there is only one entity that has been released yet, this has not been utilised in any extended way at this moment. The role of the related and linked information object is given in the role attribute, i.e. a document might be a 'deliverable of' the project and a person might be the 'author of' a document. For MXD records only the organisation entity is required, as a document published by an organisation, as is often the case with reports. The most frequent scenario is that the organisation element is describing the affiliation of an author, <person>.

DDF-MXD operates with an extensive set of vocabularies that enforces data providers to use it or map their vocabularies to the DDF-MXD standard. Insisting on the use of controlled vocabularies through XML schema validation of the used syntax enables the development of useful search and filter features.

The vocabularies are under constant development in discussion with the Danish data-providers. Especially the controlled vocabulary for document types is extensive. Each document type can also be categorised with a research indicator that indicates whether the documents are reviewed, peer reviewed or not and the scope of the document whether the level of the document is Scientific, Educational, Popular, Administrative or not determined at all. Details on the vocabularies can be found in the documentation for DDF-MXD.

In addition to the classic bibliographic elements found in the <publication> element, there is also a digital object container that includes information about objects related to the document, typically full-text. This solution is seen as a temporary and pragmatic solution for handling the increasing number of full-texts archived in the local repositories and at the same time enables better exposure of the full-texts in the DDF front end. The digital object container allows defining the role of the full-text, i.e. pre-print, post-print and publisher version, and accessibility in open access, campus access or no public access. The container can be repeated and different versions of a document can be related to the record. This is not in line with the DRIVER Guidelines[67], but should be seen as a result of the fact that the Danish repositories are CRIS and Institutional Repositories in one. In the Danish CRIS, it was preferred that authors register their research as soon as possible – in the best case in the process of writing – and this is why drafts are registered and versions are preserved in the system over time until they are finally published. This avoids duplicates, which is important in research assessments based on numbers from the CRIS databases.

---

[67] http://www.DRIVER-support.eu/managers.html (last visit on November 21st, 2008).

The Danish government has effectuated its globalisation strategy over the last couple of years, thus decreasing the number of research institutions by merging institutions into fewer bigger universities[68]. The government has increased the funding of research, while at the same time deciding that these resources should be in competition and allocated to the universities on the basis of indicators such as cooperation with private companies, number of PhD-students, patents, time-to-complete student degrees, institutions' communication with the surrounding society (Price 2008: 178). These indicators will be weighed, but the distribution of these weights has not been specified yet. It is certain that one of the central indicators will be the so-called bibliometric research indicator.

The bibliometric research indicator will monitor the research output in publications from researchers at Danish universities. The output will be classified into five different publication types:

- Monographs;
- Articles in peer reviewed journals;
- Contributions to monographs/anthologies;
- Patents;
- PhD's and doctoral theses.

Articles will be classified into 'A' and 'B' journals. This classification of journals is done by a number of research domain groups.

The Danish Agency for Science, Technology and Innovation (DASTI)[69] is responsible for the implementation of the research indicator model. DASTI has decided to use the infrastructure that the universities already have implemented. The CRIS/IR systems that have been used by most universities for years are thus well integrated into the universities' information flows and research assessment. As a result, DASTI is able to overcome the major hurdle of implementing a new system, especially a system that would intrude into the activities of highly educated and independent staff members, as academics are.

---

[68] http://www.globalisering.dk/page.dsp?area=52 (last visit on November 21st, 2008).

[69] http://en.fi.dk (last visit on November 21st, 2008).

Danish national system for research publication dissemination & statistics

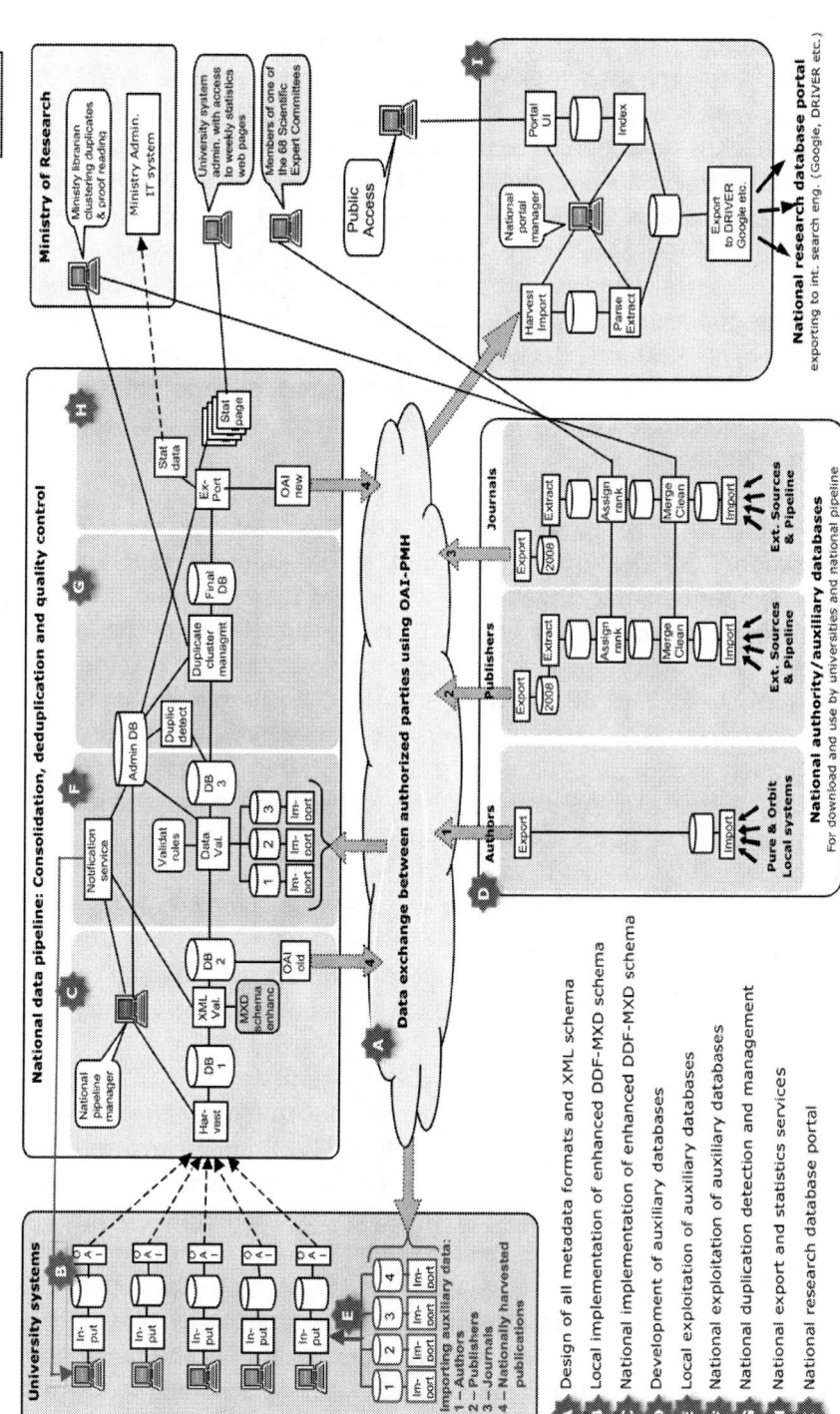

Figure 18. Danish national system for research

The requirements of DASTI in connection to the development of the Danish Research Indicator model builds fundamentally on the existing infrastructure used by the National Danish Research Database. It will harvest data based on an enhanced DDF-MXD exchange format. It will secure better bibliographic metadata and author identification by providing central authority databases as a service to the local repositories [D, see Figure 18]. It will secure a stronger and more detailed central validation that includes machine and human validation and de-duplication [C, F, G]. It will provide statistical data to the Ministry of Science, Technology and Innovation [H]. It will finally provide quality-controlled and de-duplicated records to the National Danish Research Database [I]. The system enters production phase ultimo 2008.

DDF-MXD is mapped to OAI DC but this has not been formalised anywhere. At the time of writing, it is planned that the project management behind the maintenance and development of the format will map MXD according to the DRIVER Guidelines in the autumn of 2008, thus providing a substantial contribution to the DRIVER infrastructure. The data will be validated automatically in the central harvester and duplicates or other rejected records will be presented to a human validator for double-checking the rejected records and returning them to the provider. This system will enter a pilot phase in 2008 and is planned to be operational in 2009.

The National Research Database will act as a Danish hub for delivering data to D-Net of DRIVER. This infrastructure will ensure that the development of metadata formats in Denmark are aligned making the alignment to DRIVER a non-issue for the local repository managers.

3.3.4 Conclusions on the Case Studies

The three case studies presented in this chapter have shown that integrating or interfacing CRIS and the DRIVER infrastructure will create synergies. The managerial focus on research assessment and the use of CRIS-like systems for making research assessments provides a real chance to increase content and metadata quality in not only the CRIS's but also the institutional repositories. Synergy means that the two systems are better and stronger together than when standing alone. These benefits are for all stakeholders in the academic information domain. Below is a list of benefits and opportunities for different stakeholders: the researcher, the university and its library, the national research portal.

Benefits and opportunities for the researcher are:
- One system for all research information;
- Reuse of information, little or no double entry of data;
- Pre-completed records, import from ISI and other sources means less work.

Benefits and opportunities for the university and university library are:
- Much better coverage of the actual research output, as research assessment equals money and therefore motivates registration in the CRIS/OAR system;
- CRIS/OAR integration also eases the implementation of OA-mandates, why just ask for metadata, why not demand the full-text;
- One system means less maintenance;
- CRIS requires SOA-like integration with other campus systems, thus ensuring reuse of existing data;
- SOA is also one of the biggest challenges in getting systems to work together. Getting the technical integration to work is one thing, ensuring the same level of data discipline in all servicing systems is another and much heavier task;
- Research assessment means that more money goes into development and maintenance of the system.

Benefits and opportunities for the national research portal are:
- More data;
- Better data;
- Increase number of OA full-texts.

Benefits and opportunities for the central government are:
- Existing accepted system means easier implementation of new requirements;
- Locally owned systems provide ownership of data and a stronger urge to ensure correct and timely registration of data.

3.4   Opportunities for DRIVER

DRIVER should not necessarily recommend integration of CRIS and repository systems, but could very likely benefit from recommending interoperability between the two information domains. Especially by endorsing the reuse of data, thus providing less work for the researchers that are providing content to repositories.

DRIVER could provide recommendations for the mapping from common CRIS formats like CERIF2008 to DRIVER Guidelines. Especially the vocabularies would be very helpful for feature data providers to the DRIVER infrastructure.

CRIS systems often also contain other information objects such as projects, persons like experts and authors, and activities like membership of editorial boards and being referee, and presentations. The relations between these entities are easily lost when converting from an internal CRIS format to DRIVER Guidelines. There could be an opportunity to use the Enhanced Publication model to represent relations between these entities.

4.   Long-term Preservation

4.1   Introduction

Scientific results, stored in various digital repositories, are not only of value for fellow researchers and other interested parties, but also for the next generations of researchers. They can build on the results of their predecessors, as has been done over the centuries. The fact that the research output is now mainly digital requires other efforts to keep the records of science accessible, be it two, ten or fifty years after publication. Keeping digital information accessible over the years is called digital preservation. The first DRIVER project published *A DRIVER's Guide to European Repositories* (Weenink *et al.*, 2008), in which two chapters explored the topic of digital preservation and digital curation in more detail and offered advice to repository managers. This information will not be repeated here. In *Long Term Preservation for Institutional Repositories* by Barbara Sierman, an overview is given of current developments related to different aspects of digital preservation. Digital preservation is an area where many people are involved in creating new solutions and it is worthwhile to give an update of the latest developments here.

The content of this chapter is slightly different from the other chapters. Apart from theory on long-term preservation of Enhanced Publications, it will give an update of the developments in long-term preservation, as a follow-up to chapter 6 in *A DRIVER's Guide to European Repositories* (Weenink *et al.*, 2008) The last part of this chapter will raise some issues related to the long term preservation of these Enhanced Publications for further discussion.

4.2   Theory of Long-Term Preservation

An Enhanced Publication differs from a common publication in the sense that an Enhanced Publication is a compound digital object that may consist of various heterogeneous, but related, web resources. Each of these web resources is an atomic entity and can be used on its own. In this discussion, it may be expected that each part of an Enhanced Publication can be referred to uniquely. The Enhanced Publication consists of the complete set of these atomic entities. The idea behind it is that the whole entity offers more than the sum of its parts. This advantage is something a repository wants to offer its audience. A Long-Term Preservation archive (LTP Archive) tries to keep this advantage available over the years, so that new generations will have the same opportunity to use and reuse the Enhanced Publication as originally intended.

This requires a new approach. In this chapter we put the question whether this kind of publications include other risks, compared to the preservation of the more 'classic' publications that LTP Archives are currently dealing with.

Several discussions within the DRIVER community led to the conclusion that Enhanced Publications need a special treatment regarding long-term preservation. This does not refer to the complexity of the digital object(s) itself and technical aspects, but to organisational matters related to the safekeeping of the Enhanced Publication.

On two main topics these publications differ from classic publications: 'shared ownership' and the 'capturing' process. The 'shared ownership' relates to the fact that parts of the Enhanced Publications might be stored in different repositories, even in different countries. Each repository has its own set of policies, legal obligations and operating routines, which affects the way a repository will govern its publications. Some parts of EP's might not even be in a repository but on a website, without a clearly defined 'owner' or 'manager'. Hence, an EP might be subject to a variety of different policies. This makes a general approach more problematic and increases the difficulty in the harvesting of an EP for an LTP Archive, as the harvesting activity needs to take the different policies into account.

In the 'capturing process' the EP is made available for long-term preservation meeting certain requirements, like structural information, and metadata. If parts of an Enhanced Publication are stored in different repositories, every part will be subject to different technical aspects, like the standards used for describing the structure of the EP or the descriptive metadata, the preservation metadata that are added. Every repository has its own standards and the LTP Archive needs to deal with this. The LTP Archive has an obligation only to store objects that are suitable for long-term preservation and will have its own standards, which might not be met by all different parts of the EP. These are the starting points for the discussion about long-term preservation of Enhanced Publications. More details and discussion points will shed light on the related organisational challenges and some recommendations will be formulated.

4.2.1 What is an Enhanced Publication?

An Enhanced Publication is a publication that is enhanced with research data, extra materials, post publication data, database records, and has an object-based structure with explicit links between the objects. An object can be (part of) an article, a data set, an image, a movie, a comment, a module or a link to information in a database.

This definition supposes that one Institutional Repository has the publication and that all the other object parts are related to this 'root publication'[70]. The same report states that parts of the compound object might be distributed over several repositories, even in different countries. Each part of the Enhanced Publication is an autonomous entity and understandable on its own.

In the field of digital preservation, the Open Archival Information System (OAIS) model is a standard, translated into a practical approach in the Trustworthy Repositories and Certification (TRAC) criteria and checklist. The starting points in these publications are the guiding principles for this chapter about long-term archiving of Enhanced Publications.

As an Enhanced Publication consists of different parts, the main question is: How do we get the different parts in different repositories into one Long-Term Preservation Archive (LTP Archive), to offer the future user this Enhanced Publication as one complete entity?

Technically speaking, it looks like the long term archiving will not lead to new problems or challenges, since EP's consist of digital objects that are autonomous entities. This does not imply that there are already satisfying solutions for long-term preservation of a database or a website. But long term preservation of EP's will have more consequences in the organisational aspect. In the list of discussion points in Paragraph 4.2.2 the predicted challenges as well as possible solutions are described and some preliminary answers are given.

---

[70] For the discussion we use this concept of a 'root' object in the Enhanced Publication. This concept is not part of the EP Model in Woutersen-Windhouwer and Brandsma (2009).

4.2.2   Enhanced Publications Discussion Points

EP ready for long term Archiving

At a certain moment someone decides that an Enhanced Publication needs to be archived for the long term and maybe moved to an LTP Archive. The manager of the repository in which the 'root' publication is stored normally will make this decision.

But if separate parts of an Enhanced Publication are stored in different repositories, is there a hierarchy between these parts/repositories? Which repository can make the decision to send the Enhanced Publication to the LTP Archive? And based on which part of the Enhanced Publication? In other words, is there a part of the Enhanced Publication that will be the catalyst for this activity? It sound reasonable to let the 'root publication' be the catalyst. In most cases this will work well. But what if an EP has related EP's? For example, if the 'root publication' the author indicated is a textual article and in the EP is also a data set related to this article. Other authors also used this data set and there are related EP's to this data set. But assume this data set is very large and important and a lot of articles are published, based on this data set? In this case, it is more logical to make the data set the 'root publication' and the catalyst for long-term preservation. However, the repository manager(s) might not have the overview to make such a decision.

For the LTP Archive, the repository manager will be the Producer (in OAIS terminology) of the Enhanced Publication, representing the original author, who is out of scope for the LTP Archive. But is the repository manager able to decide if and when the EP as a whole, inclusive the different parts of it, is ready for long term archiving, whilst at the same time the author might still be adding parts to this Enhanced Publication in other repositories?

These matters should be solved before the LTP Archive receives the Enhanced Publication, as the LTP Archives are not able to make this decision.

A solution could be that at a certain moment the repository manager decides that this EP is complete 'as is' and offers the EP to the LTP Archive, similar to harvesting websites. This will require a versioning mechanism.

Completeness of EP

An Enhanced Publication may consist of parts that are in one repository and other parts in another repository. Each part however, needs to be autonomous. If the EP will be collected for long-term preservation, how does the Producer, i.e. the repository manager, know that every part of the EP is complete and finalised? Does this even have to be the case? Or should there be a mechanism to decide which parts of the Enhanced Publication are ready for long-term preservation? As an Enhanced Publication could have additions over the years, the object model should allow versioning, and the LTP Archive should also allow for this. For the future user, it is important that there are references from the first version to later versions.

Legal and technical Aspects of Harvesting and Storage

Is the Producer, the repository manager of the 'root publication' allowed to negotiate with an LTP Archive about archiving parts of Enhanced Publication that are stored in other repositories than his own? Can he negotiate on behalf of other repositories? Negotiating could mean making agreements with the LTP Archive on access rights, on preservation actions, on services on the data in the LTP Archive. If the repository manager is not allowed to act on behalf of other repositories, where parts of the EP are stored, is there a possibility that he, as the Producer archives the persistent identifiers of the missing components? With this information in the LTP Archive, the future users might be able to find the missing parts via the web.

Besides that, an LTP Archive will have its own policies on the objects to collect and it might decide not to archive certain parts of the Enhanced Publication if these are in conflict with its policies. This might implicate that the whole EP is not kept as it originally was published and intended. This has consequences for the future users.

Representation Information

The LTP Archive needs to gather sufficient information about the digital object to be able to preserve it for the long term. This implies significant properties and representation information. All parts of the Enhanced Publication need to be accompanied by this information, otherwise long-term storage in the Enhanced Publication will be difficult. Although there are tools, like DROID[71] and JHOVE[72], where part of this

---

[71] http://droid.sourceforge.net/wiki/index.php/Introduction (last access on December 12th, 2008).

information could be extracted automatically, this is not an option for all required metadata. So it is important to agree on a minimal set of metadata. The Producer is the one who should monitor the presence of this minimal set. But will the Producer have sufficient power to impose this? Otherwise the Enhanced Publications, or parts of it, will be in danger of being no longer accessible by absence of descriptive metadata, or unusable in the future by having passwords.

This topic is related to the requirement that the LTP Archive identifies properties of the object it will preserve (TRAC)[73]. The producer in this case will be the spokesman for all the parts of the Enhanced Publication and should agree so with the relevant repositories.

Designated Community
The LTP Archive should have a clear view on the Designated Community of the Enhanced Publications in order to be able to keep the EP's accessible and usable for future users. As this concerns research information, the objects in the original repository might originate from different research communities. The LTP Archive needs the essential information about these communities, as it is likely that for the long term the Designated Community will be similar with the original research community. The Producer would be the one giving this information to the LTP Archive and describe this in the agreement. But does the Producer have sufficient knowledge of these different Designated Communities related to the EP's to serve them right?

Control over the Content
The LTP Archive needs to have sufficient control over the content (TRAC). One of the areas related to this, is the question of file formats and software used to create the parts of the EP. As this concerns research information, parts of the Enhanced Publication might be created with dedicated software lacking publicly available information. Such information is vital for long-term archiving of the objects. Is the Producer able to retrieve this information, and maybe the related software itself, if parts of the Enhanced Publication are beyond his mandate? If not, the LTP Archive should indicate that they cannot guarantee the LTP of these publications by adding a certain preservation level, indicating this.

---

[72] http://hul.harvard.edu/jhove/ (last access on December 12th, 2008).
[73] http://www.crl.edu/PDF/trac.pdf (last access on December 12th, 2008).

Future Users

The future user should get the Enhanced Publication he expects, so if an LTP archive starts to archive these EP's, all concerns in relation to rights and copyrights should be established and clear to that future user. This could also imply that certain parts of the EP will not be visible to him.

Authenticity is an important factor, especially as parts of the publication might originate from different repositories. Authenticity of the separate objects in the Enhanced Publication must be guaranteed.

Distribution of LTP Archives

If the LTP archiving of the Enhanced Publication is divided over more than one archive the involved archives must reach a mutual agreement on archiving principles, policies, ingest checks and preservation actions for this collection. An example of this is the Dutch situation, where the research data are stored at Data Archiving and Networking Services (DANS), the publications at the KB, unless they consist of audio or sound material, in which case they are stored at the 'Nederlands Instituut voor Beeld en Geluid'.

The LTP Archives

The LTP Archive should have the right of preservation actions on every part of the Enhanced Publication if the LTP Archive thinks it is necessary. This is partly a matter of legal and technical aspects that should be taken care of. If parts of the EP do not fit in the Archives SIP/AIP definition and the EP is a publication distributed over different repositories, who is the contact for the LTP Archive to discuss and solve this? This has to do with ownership and mandate.

Persistent Identifiers

According to Verhaar (2009) Enhanced Publications must be available as web resources that can be referenced via a URI. The same goes for its components and it must be possible to secure the long-term preservation of Enhanced Publications. Hence all the components of an Enhanced Publication must be uniquely referenced using persistent identifiers in order to make them available for LTP. The resolver of the EP will have to point to the different URI's of the components.

Who will maintain the resolver for the URI's in the long term? The resolver will be the only means for a future user to find a reference to a component if this is not available in the repository archives. The unique persistent identifier is so important, that one could wonder whether an

LTP Archive should not be very strict on this and not allow ingest of EP's without a persistent identifier. As it is likely that there will never be only one method for unique persistent identifiers, the LPT Archive needs to take special care that it can check the validity of the references and the different persistent identifiers' methods used.

4.2.3 Recommendations on long-term Archiving of EP's

In the previous paragraphs several questions are put forward with respect to the long-term preservation of Enhanced Publications. To most of the questions there is no direct answer and they need further discussion. Because of the complexity of this material, we recommend the following:

- As long-term archiving of EPs of which various parts are distributed over several repositories entails extra complications, especially regarding legal issues, it would be wise to start on a small scale. For example, thinking about procedures related to long-term preservation of Enhanced Publications where the 'root' object and the related objects are all present in one single repository, under one mandate;
- A mechanism should be created that automatically derives the status of the EP or parts of it, so that a repository has a way to decide which EP is ready for sending to an LTP Archive. For example a status 'complete' would then mean 'ready for harvesting for long-term preservation';
- For all Enhanced Publications, a minimal set of metadata will be required, including a persistent identifier. This set of preservation metadata will be larger than suggested by Verhaar (2009) because information like file format (MIME type) is not detailed enough for LTP Archives. Additional data are file format version, date of creation and software name and version, used to create the object. Some information might be used for digital preservation, like the time stamp, as this gives information about the date the publication was created. In times of emergency, this could be vital information to determine which kind of software was used to create the object and so helps to find the rendering application;
- Legal and copyright issues need to be solved before EP's are sent to an LTP Archive;
- LTP Archives should develop a policy about which LTP Archive will store which kind of material and coordinate their approaches.

4.3   Update on digital Preservation Topics

4.3.1   File format Services

Determining the file format and version of the digital object is a prerequisite for long-term preservation of the object. Several initiatives support LTP Archives in this activity. New developments regarding JHOVE, GDFR (Global Digital Format Registry) and AONSII are of interest for DRIVER II.

JHOVE2

The *DRIVER's Guide for Institutional Repositories* mentions several drawbacks of JHOVE, the metadata extraction tool, for example its limitation to a set of only twelve file formats it can handle, the large quantity of metadata it generates and the lack of documentation. New developments might change this criticism. JHOVE will be succeeded by a new initiative JHOVE2. Three US-based organisations, the California Digital Library, Portico, a long-term archive for scholarly literature, and Stanford University together will work on a new release of JHOVE and they will draw lessons from the points of criticism. The project will last two years and is funded by the Library of Congress under its National Digital Information Infrastructure Preservation Program (NDIIPP) (Abrams *et al.*, 2008). JHOVE2 aims to incorporate major improvements, like a new architecture, better performance and new features. Format characterisation will include validation, identification, which are both available in JHOVE, but also feature extraction, meaning the extraction of significant properties and the support of assessment of the object, based on locally defined policies. The project will be finished in 2010.

GDFR

As with many initiatives in digital preservation, once the first results are there, the question of sustainability is raised. This is currently the situation with the Global Digital Format Registry (GDFR). GDFR was supported by the Mellon Foundation to create a software platform, but now a community around the governance of the registry needs to be set up. There is no doubt that the GDFR fulfils a need, as the knowledge of file formats is crucial in digital preservation, but the question is now who will participate in the community, to test the beta release of the software, what is the relation with the PRONOM Registry of The National Archives in the UK, to name a few[74].

---

[74] http://www.gdfr.info/index.html (last access on November 22nd, 2008).

AONSII

Many file formats have only have a limited lifespan, although this may cover many years. For preservation purposes, it is not only important to know the file format of the digital object but also when it becomes obsolete. The reasoning behind this is that a file format that becomes less popular will have less support from the supplier and other third parties will not support the use of the file format in their software. The file format then becomes a risk for the repository, and a consequence will be that objects are no longer accessible or usable. To manage this risk, some warning system in the preservation community would be useful.

The Australian Partnership for Sustainable Repositories (APSR) released in 2007 a beta version of the Format Notification and Obsolescence Tool (AONSII)[75], which is a successor of AONSI, developed in cooperation with the National Library of Australia. It aims to be a platform-independent, downloadable tool that uses the file format information in international registries like Pronom and GDFR. When monitoring the status of file formats in a repository, the tool will provide information about these file formats, based on the information available in these registries. This information will help the repository manager to decide which actions to take.

4.3.2 Persistent Identifiers

Digital objects must have a persistent identifier, so researchers are able to identify the digital source over the years correctly. The actual use of persistent identifiers can be improved and there are initiatives to create the necessary infrastructure for PI's.

PILIN

One of the objectives of the Australian PILIN (Persistent Identifier Linking Infrastructure) project was to strengthen Australia's ability to use global identifier infrastructure and they succeeded as the project team concluded in their final report. Based on the Handle technology, the project investigated further developments related to the use of persistent identifiers. Persistent identifiers are crucial for digital objects, without a persistent identifier it will not be possible to locate an object over the years. This is not a matter of technology only, but requires an infrastructure with a "long-term governance and policy support at

---

[75] http://www.apsr.edu.au/aons2 (last access on November 22nd, 2008).

institutional, sectoral and global levels"[76]. The project investigated several aspects and produced a variety of results, including software, policy guidelines and impact reports. It needs further funding to make the results ready for a real life business environment.

4.3.3 Archival Concepts / Repository Models

The OAIS Reference model acts as a standard in the digital preservation community. As this is a conceptual model, it needs to be translated into practical implementations. One of the initiatives to investigate this is within a project that is funded by the European Commission.

OAIS

The basic reference model for digital preservation environments is the OAIS (Open Archival Information System). In compliance with ISO and CCSDS procedures, a standard must be reviewed every five years and a decision made to reaffirm, modify, or withdraw the existing standard. The Reference Model for the OAIS standard was approved as CCSDS 650.0-B-1 in January 2002 and as ISO standard 14721 in 2003. A comment period was therefore announced in 2006[77]. The publication of the updated OAIS reference model is expected for January 2009 (Rusbridge, 2008).

SHAMAN

Concepts for preservation environments evolve only slowly. This meets the general expectations on digital preservation. While for different reasons a change of the underlying technology and implementation of an archive may be considered as necessary, it does not seem very trustworthy if an archive would change its overall strategy or structure at the same rate. This is one of the ideas for archival concepts, which has received more attention over the last years through some test-bed activities. So-called persistent archives are considered necessary to ensure long-term preservation. The aim is to describe and maintain the entire preservation environment context, i.e. the management policies, the preservation processes, the logical namespaces and the persistent state information, while every of its components may change and be migrated to a new preservation environment. To realise such a comprehensive 'Theory of Preservation', the National Archives and

---

[76] See https://www.pilin.net.au (last access on November 22nd, 2008) and PILIN Team (2007).

[77] http://nost.gsfc.nasa.gov/isoas/oais-rm-review.html (last access on November 22nd, 2008).

Records Administration (NARA) and the EU project SHAMAN[78] implement persistent archive test beds (Watry, 2007; Smith and Moore, 2007).

CASPAR

The aim of the EU project Cultural, Artistic and Scientific knowledge for Preservation, Access and Retrieval (CASPAR)[79] is to provide an infrastructure to support an implementation of the OAIS. Two main developments of CASPAR are worth mentioning: the OAIS-based preservation-aware storage and their research to support the management and preservation of the OAIS representation information.

Preservation-aware storage is storage hardware that supports OAIS functions for metadata like representation information, provenance and fixity. An example is the computation of fixity checksums, which can be directly performed by the preservation-aware storage instead of reading the data from normal storage, computing the checksum on a separate CPU and writing the checksum back to the storage. CASPAR anticipates that *"preservation systems will be more robust and have less probability for data corruption or loss if they offload preservation related functionality to the storage layer."* (CASPAR, 2007a: 53).

Representation Information is an important concept of the OAIS. It is the information necessary to understand the archived data. It must be generated to organise the preservation process. Examples are the description of the file format in which the data is saved, or a dictionary, which explains the terms of a document. But the representation information itself relies on the background knowledge of a community, which may change over time. Therefore, additional representation information will be necessary. CASPAR defines a few major components to solve this central issue with regard to these challenges and will develop registries, creation tools and interfaces for representation information (CASPAR, 2007b: pp. 15-19, 21-26, 33).

---

[78] SHAMAN: Sustaining Heritage Access Through Multivalent Archiving, http://shaman-ip.eu (last access on November 22nd, 2008).
[79] http://www.casparpreserves.eu (last access on November 22nd, 2008).

4.4　Metadata

4.4.1　PREMIS

One of the most important standards for long-term preservation is PREMIS (PREservation Metadata: Implementation Strategies). The PREMIS Data Dictionary for Preservation Metadata defines *"a core set of implementable preservation metadata, broadly applicable across a wide range of digital preservation contexts and supported by guidelines and recommendations for creation, management, and use"* (PREMIS Editorial Committee, 2008) and was published first in May 2005. A substantially updated version was released in March 2008 as a result of broad feedback.

The major changes are (Lavoie, 2008):

- *Data model.* The semantic units of PREMIS belong to five different entities: Intellectual Entities, Objects, Events, Rights, and Agent. These entities have different relationships: *"In PREMIS 2.0, relationships in the data model have been generalised to exhibit bi-directionality in all cases, including those involving Agents."* (Lavoie, 2008).

- *Rights Entity.* The semantic units for the rights entity have been revised and expanded.

- *Significant Properties and Preservation Level.* A more detailed description of significant properties and preservation levels is possible.

- *Extensibility.* A formal mechanism for extensions of seven semantic units has been introduced.

The separate schemas for each entity have been merged into one schema. PREMIS is the major metadata standard concerning digital preservation. But PREMIS alone does not seem sufficient for the long-term preservation management of digital assets. It has to be supplemented by different types of metadata like descriptive, technical and structural metadata. A common choice is to implement PREMIS within METS, the Metadata Encoding and Transmission Standard, a container format for other metadata standards, which provide structural metadata. But this requires some important decisions since PREMIS and METS overlap. To support this task, a specific guideline has been developed as part of the PREMIS maintenance activity (Guenter, 2008; Guidelines, 2008).

4.4.2 INSPECT

What makes the preservation of a digital object a success? This apparently simple question turns out to be quite tricky. As it is nearly impossible to preserve a digital object in every aspect, for a rational preservation strategy losses in less important aspects have to be accepted. 'Significant properties' is the common term for those aspects of a digital object, which have to be preserved for a Designated Community. Significant properties are usually divided in five different categories: content, context, structure, appearance and behaviour. The same digital object can have different significant properties depending on the purpose of the preservation. For an art historian, the appearance of an object will be much more important than the content, while for other researchers or readers it may be the other way around. To support the identification of significant properties of digital objects in a structured way the Joint Information System Committee (JISC) funded INSPECT[80] project has published a framework (Knight, 2008). Besides proposing a methodology, it provides an initial analysis of some file types.

4.5 Preservation Strategies

4.5.1 The PLANETS Plato Tool

Long-term preservation of digital objects needs preservation actions to keep objects accessible and usable over the years. These actions are part of an organisation's preservation planning, the main topic of the European project PLANETS (Preservation and Long-term Access through NETworked Services)[81].

One of the results of this project will be the Preservation Planning tool PLATO, an automated decision tool, based on the PLANETS preservation planning methodology. The tool assists organisations to define their requirements, collection profiles and other essential information for preservation actions. It will evaluate this input and will give a recom-

---

[80]http://www.jisc.ac.uk/whatwedo/programmes/programme_rep_pres/inspect.as px (last access on November 22nd, 2008).
[81] http://www.planets-project.eu (last access on November 22nd, 2008).

mendation for optimal preservation action for that particular collection[82].

4.5.2 Developments in Emulation

Hardware emulation is the preservation action in which the original hardware architecture is mimicked through software. This supports the process of bringing digital objects back to life in their own environment without changing the object itself, but by changing the environment. The Dioscuri emulator, which is especially designed for long-term preservation and of which the first release was launched in 2007, was upgraded in 2008 to a 32-bit version. This emulator is available as an open source tool[83].

For the actual rendering of a digital artefact, the emulation tool only will not be enough. Information is needed about dependencies on the original hardware and software environment. Besides that, the original software should be available. And there should be a mechanism to match these requirements so the emulator can work properly. In the Planets project, the DIOSCURI emulator will be integrated in the Planets framework as a remote emulator service, offering the end-user a solution to render his objects, instead of just a tool. The first results are expected in 2009 and will be part of the official end result of the Planets suite. The work done on emulation in Planets will be extended in a new project KEEP (Keeping Emulation Environments Portable), with support of the European Commission. The goal of this project is to build an emulation access platform, where several emulators will be available in order to allow end-users to access digital objects in their own environment. This access platform will be designed to be sustainable by making it portable to a wide range of computers in present and future. The platform will also be extensible to allow new emulators and additional services for information reuse to be integrated as easy as possible. Another area that KEEP will cover is offering means to transfer data from outdated computer media carriers to new carriers or storage devices, for example disk images. This can be helpful for precious

---

[82] Although the final version of this tool will be delivered at the end of the project in 2010, organizations can have a preview:
http://www.ifs.tuwien.ac.at/dp/plato/intro.html (last access on November 22nd, 2008).
[83] website Dioscuri: http://dioscuri.sourceforge.net (last access on November 22nd, 2008).

digital data, hidden in cupboards and desks, on obsolete hardware, and with vital information.

The creation of a software archive for operating and application software is crucial for emulation, but, at this moment, such functionality is not yet available. One of the reasons for this originates in the unsolved challenges with regard to legal aspects of preserving and reusing software for long-term preservation purposes. The KEEP project will also investigate the consequences of establishing a software archive.

4.6   Organisational Aspects of Digital Preservation

Digital preservation of a set of objects requires an organisation that is able to commit to these tasks for a long time. Initiatives like the above-mentioned Trustworthy Audit and Certification Checklist will assist the organisations. Over the last year there have been a few new developments in the area of the organisational aspects of digital preservation.

4.6.1   Keeping Research Data safe
A major report on cost estimates of digital preservation was released by Charles Beagrie Limited on behalf of the Higher Education Funding Council for England (HEFCE), UK. It provides a framework for cost estimates, lists key cost variables, activities, reports on case studies at UK universities and gives recommendations for future work (Beagrie *et al.*, 2008a).

LIFE2 project
Another major activity regarding the costs of digital preservation is the sequel of the Life Cycle Information for E-Literature (LIFE)[84] project. The LIFE project used a lifecycle model for electronic publications to estimate costs and identified different cost elements for each lifecycle stage. LIFE2 refined the model of the first project and took several different areas into account, e.g. the costs for preserving material in institutional repositories, for preserving material using an external service and a comparison of the costs for sustaining digital or print material.

---

[84] http://www.life.ac.uk (last access on November 22nd, 2008).

The general formula provided for cost estimates is:

$$L(T) = C + Aq(T) + I(T) + M(T) + BP(T) + CP(T) + AC(T)$$

L=Complete lifecycle cost over time 0 to T, C=Creation, Aq=Acquisition, I=Ingest, M=Metadata Creation, BP=Bit-stream Preservation, CP=Content Preservation, and Ac=Access (Ayris *et al.*, 2008: 32).

All of these lifecycle stages are further divided into sub processes which are described in detail in the final report and for which the case studies provide real life cost estimates. Nevertheless the LIFE2 project team sees still demand for refining the model in order to become predictive.

PLATTER

Several initiatives are currently working on audit and certification of trustworthy repositories, like TRAC, DRAMBORA and Nestor. Together they formulated the ten core principles of trust. These basic principles were input for the PLATTER tool (Planning Tool for Trusted Electronic Repositories)[85], a tool especially developed to help organisations starting with digital preservation, to implement these principles and being able to meet the audit and certification requirements. The tool is the result of an initiative of Digital Preservation Europe (2008) and can be found online[86].

Preservation Policies JISC

This JISC funded a study on digital preservation policies that aims to provide an outline model (Beagrie *et al.*, 2008b). The target groups of this report are universities with their digital collections. Long-term access of these collections can only be guaranteed if there are policies and procedures in place, based on which preservation activities can be performed. This report is based on desk research of existing literature, policies of other institutions, not only research institutions, but also libraries, archives and data centres, and on case studies. It offers practical assistance for Institutional Repositories.

---

[85] Published in 2008, see http://roda.iantt.pt/pt/node/240 (last access on November 22nd, 2008).

[86] http://www.digitalpreservationeurope.eu/platter (last access on November 22nd, 2008).

DANS Data Seal of Approval

The Data Seal of Approval is a set of seventeen quality guidelines for digital research data developed by The Data Archiving and Networked Services (DANS) (Sesink *et al.*, 2008). DANS is the Dutch organisation responsible for providing permanent access to research data from the Humanities and Social Sciences. The guidelines are for the producers, repositories and users of research data and are a derived and distilled version of other guidelines and checklists like TRAC, DRAMBORA or the RIN reports mentioned below[87].

Legal Issues

When preserving digital material, it might be necessary to perform actions on the digital objects in order to keep the object accessible and usable. These actions might conflict with copyright laws. Preserving organisations are not always sure whether they are allowed to perform the necessary tasks. Is it allowed to make multiple copies of a work for preservation purposes? Or to migrate works to a new technological format, thus creating a new manifestation of the original object? National laws are often not updated for the digital age, and if they are, this aspect is often not tackled. Recently, a study (International Study, 2008) drew attention to this problem and concluded with a set of joint recommendations to provide guidelines for national copyright and related right laws.

4.7 Scientific Data and digital Research Infrastructures

Traditional memory institutions like libraries, archives and museums are probably the technology drivers in the area of long-term preservation, but they are certainly not the only ones with a demand for digital preservation. In many areas of science data, intensive research is established or on the rise. Digital data are a resource and a result of modern science, which needs to be preserved for different reasons. Climate research is not possible without data from previous climate observations, which are obviously not reproducible. Other data may be reproducible theoretically, but the result of such experiments is so expensive that this is practically infeasible. Moreover, as fraud of research results has repeatedly been reported, the preservation of

---

[87] More information on http://www.datasealofapproval.org (last access on November 22nd, 2008).

scientific data may also be instrumental for later verifications of claimed results.

While the demand of science for long-term preservation of data may be evident, it is far from obvious how this should be organised. For publications and analogue artefacts, the traditional memory institutions will traditionally be considered responsible. The emerging memory institutions like community specific data centres have to create their workflows from scratch and cannot build on traditional knowledge. Additional challenges are concerned with data flood, research specific data and customised data formats.

4.7.1   PARSE.insight

PARSE.insight is a two-year European project, started in 2008, that will investigate the practice and awareness of digital preservation in the European research community. Research institutions create masses of valuable data, and it is important for the reuse of these data in an e-infrastructure that these data are taken care of for the long term. The project will come with an overview of the current state of affairs and formulate recommendations on how to stimulate the long term archiving of research data in order to prevent unwanted loss. Based on their findings, the PARSE.Insight project will advise the European Commission on this topic.

4.7.2   Stewardship of digital Research Data

The Research Information Network (RIN) produced a framework of principles and guidelines called 'Stewardship of digital research data'[88] (Research Information Network, 2008a). Its core is five very high-level principles, which serve as a starting point for further developments. Although all principles are important to consider for ensuring the long-term availability of research data, the fifth principle explicitly states the need to preserve research data for future generations.

4.7.3   Dealing with Data

In 2007, Liz Lyon (from UKOLN, at the University of Bath) published a report for JISC about how to organise the preservation, access and reuse of research data. The report (Lyon, 2007) is an elaboration of the RIN framework mentioned above and defines, as the subtitle says, the 'roles, rights, responsibilities and relationships' of actors like scientists, institutions, data centres, users and funders. It is based on a series of

---

[88] http://www.rin.ac.uk/data-principles (last access on November 22nd, 2008).

workshops and interviews with stakeholders of funding organisations, data services and repositories whose findings are presented. Besides that, it gives a comprehensive set of recommendations to JISC.

4.7.4 To share or not to share

The RIN report 'To Share or not to Share'[89] (Research Information Network, 2008b) primarily addresses data publication, not long-term preservation. But the question of data publication shares a similar perspective with the question of long-term preservation. How can research data created in one context be reused in another context? The report gathers the results of extensive interviews with over 100 researchers in the area of Classics, Social and Public Health Sciences, Astronomy, Chemical crystallography, Genomics, Systems Biology, Rural Economy and Land Use and Climate Science. Topics are, amongst other things, the state of the art in data creation and curation, publishing, access and reuse of data. This is very interesting for DRIVER II in the context of EP's.

4.7.5 Data Audit Framework

The Data Audit Framework is a method developed by HATII at the University of Glasgow together with the Digital Curation Center and is an implementation of one of Liz Lyon's above-mentioned recommendations in Dealing with Data. The framework defines a workflow for institutions to assist them in answering some basic but essential questions about their data collections (Jones et al., 2008). Paper tools are provided and an online tool is announced.

4.7.6 UKRDS

The UK Research Data Service (UKRDS)[90] feasibility study is a joint project between RLUK (the Consortium of Research Libraries in the UK and Ireland), and RUGIT (the Russell Group IT Directors Group). Serco Consulting in partnership with Charles Beagrie Limited and Grant Thornton were appointed as consultants for the study. Its objective is to assess the feasibility and costs of developing and maintaining a national shared digital research data service for UK Higher Education sector. The recently released UKRDS Interim Report is an early draft from the feasibility stage, intended as a working draft of the Feasibility Study report. The interim report includes an initial analysis of a survey carried out of some 700 researchers at four case study sites (Oxford, Leeds,

---

[89] http://www.rin.ac.uk/data-publication (last access on November 22nd, 2008).
[90] http://www.ukrds.ac.uk (last access on November 22nd, 2008).

Bristol, Leicester), regarding their current storage provision and future requirements (UKRDS, 2008).

4.8   Opportunities for DRIVER

Repositories that take care of Enhanced Publications will need to take extra measures to make theses publications ready for long-term preservation. Apart from technical measures, like adding a minimal set of metadata, such as file format, version, software used, date of creation and adding persistent identifiers, they also need to take organisational steps to solve legal issues, streamline the information regarding the individual parts of the Enhanced Publication, determine the status of the separate parts as finished, in progress, not for publication, and establish ownership. Guidelines which provide advice for these organisational issues and LTP requirements for the object models of Enhanced Publications are worth developing as an integral part of the DRIVER Guidelines for European repositories.

Some repositories have ambitions to take care of long-term preservation themselves. Other repositories will send their content to LTP Archives. In both cases, the repositories should be aware of the developments in the digital preservation community to be able to implement the right measures in time, so that their digital objects will be prepared for long-term preservation. The way a digital object is created, i.e. the file format chosen, the software used, and the accompanying metadata, strongly influences the chances that the digital object will survive. In contrast to LTP Archives, repository managers can, to a certain degree, influence these choices. If the repository managers are aware of this by having a basic knowledge of digital preservation, they can offer better advice to the researchers. DRIVER can improve the awareness of repository managers about LTP by providing best practices and guidelines through the DRIVER support site and country correspondents, as well as by participating in repository or digital library conferences on LTP, to underline the importance of an efficient LTP strategy for European repositories.

Repositories that take care of Enhanced Publications will have to take extra measures to make theses publications ready for long-term preservation. Apart from technical measures, like adding a minimal set of metadata such as file format, version, software used, date of creation and adding Persistent Identifiers, they also need to take organisational steps to solve legal issues, streamline the information regarding the individual parts of the Enhanced Publication. They will have to determine the status of the separate parts as finished, in progress, or not for publication, and the ownership. DRIVER can push this minimal set of data to the repositories through the DRIVER Guidelines and make sure that the structure of EP's is preserved through these measures.

The DRIVER community should be aware of the developments in the digital preservation community to be able to implement the right measures in time, so that their digital objects will be prepared for long-term preservation in the LTP Archive.

PART 3: Framework for Interoperablity

Magchiel Bijsterbosch, Karen Van Godtsenhoven ,
Patrick Hochstenbach, Rosemary Russell,
Maurice Vanderfeesten

5. New Standards, Formats and Evolutions

5.1 Introduction

Focus is here on the output of structural metadata, since this is very important in the DRIVER context of harvesting and aggregating of Enhanced Publications. Descriptive metadata standards are well known and widely agreed upon, e.g. XML-based element sets such as MODS[91] and Dublin Core (DC). This chapter will deal with structural metadata, which can be found on a deeper level than the descriptive metadata, and determine the way the descriptive metadata are linked to the object. Structural metadata schemes are important because they express the way the object is structured and how it relates to its descriptive metadata. This is important for the exchange of records by harvesters and aggregators, especially in the context of Enhanced Publications, the focus of DRIVER II, where metadata are associated with different files that 'live' at different locations. What are the options to get easier access not only to metadata but also to the publications? From a technology viewpoint there are five routes available.

5.1.1 Classification
The following classification is not strict but shows the direction into which technologies tend to move.

Envelopes, compound objects or packaging formats
It is very hard to come up with good names, because, depending on the context, they have multiple usages. These formats provide access to the metadata, structural data, identifiers, and sometimes also binary streams of publications all in one package (envelope). They tend to give a complete description and have ideally no external dependencies. Examples are METS, MPEG21-DIDL (e.g. Bekaert *et al.*, 2003), LOM/IMS[92], ODF packages, OOXML Open Packaging Convention, Open eBook Packaging Format[93].

---

[91] http://www.loc.gov/standards/mods (last access on November 23rd, 2008).

[92] http://wiki.cetis.ac.uk/What_is_IEEE_LOM/IMS_LRM (last access on November 23rd, 2008).

[93] http://www.openebook.org (last access on November 23rd, 2008).

Overlays, maps, feeds

These formats provide an overlay on top of an existing network of internet resources. They tend to group references to resources, identify them and describe the content, structure and relations of all parts. Examples are: RDF, ORE[94], POWDER, SWAP, TopicMaps[95], Atom (Nottingham and Sayre, 2005), RSS[96], Sitemaps.org[97], ROR[98].

Embedding, or extending existing resources

Here, no new resources are introduced on the network, but existing resources are enriched by adding semantic annotations. Hence, the PDF link is embedded in splash page with special code highlighting its location. Examples are: RDFa (Adida *et al.*, 2008), Microformats, XMP (Adobe, 2005).

New/old publishing formats

With new HTML versions and XML publishing formats, a whole new range of open semantically rich and crawlable documents becomes available. Examples: HTML5 (Hickson and Hyatt, 2008), XHTML (W3C HTML Working Group, 2002), ODF (Brauer *et al.* 2005), OOXML.

Web services

Arguably, a bit of a catchall. The other four formats are rather static, there is no interaction needed with a dynamic service to extract all the information needed. For web services, one needs to add API's in addition to OAI-PMH on top of digital repositories to answer questions from agents on the content of your collections. The web services world is 'divided' in two movements, 'Resource-Oriented-Architectures' and 'Service-Oriented-Architectures'. Examples are: GData[99], O.K.I.[100].

This classification is used as a 'grid' for this chapter on interoperability. For each classification, a theoretical part, case studies and opportunities for DRIVER regarding integration will be provided.

---

[94] http://www.openarchives.org/ore (last access on November 23rd, 2008).

[95] http://www.topicmaps.org (last access on November 23rd, 2008).

[96] http://cyber.law.harvard.edu/rss/rss.html (last access on November 23rd, 2008).

[97] http://www.sitemaps.org (last access on November 23rd, 2008).

[98] http://www.rorweb.com (last access on November 23rd, 2008).

[99] http://code.google.com/apis/gdata/overview.html (last access on November 23rd, 2008).

[100] http://okiproject.org (last access on December 4th, 2008).

5.1.2 Definitions and Framework of Interoperability

Sharing distributed resources including articles, data sets, images (Enhanced Publications) and other types of records requires an interoperable system on different levels, e.g. record level, metadata level, repository level, protocol level.

The Institute of Electrical and Electronics Engineers (1990) defines interoperability as the ability of two or more systems or components to exchange information and to use the information that has been exchanged.

This way, the definition stresses both the usability and interpretability of the information. Reuse of information is very important in this context. Sharing metadata requires agreements on four topics[101]: semantics, syntax, structure and protocol.

Semantics

What is the meaning behind metadata assertions? Because 'meaning' is a psychological concept, it is harder for machines/computers to interpret this the same way. The focus of the Dublin Core effort has been to promote those shared meanings and makes them sharable. Semantics, in this sense, is about agreeing on meaningful elements like author, publisher, and date.

Syntax

The syntax defines how two machines can communicate, and how metadata assertions can be 'packaged' in order to move from one machine to another, after which they can be unpacked and be parsed by machine logic in order to be displayed in a human-readable form. The syntax makes sure that the meaning stays unchanged throughout this transfer. E.g. in an RDF document, syntax is interpreted as the serialisation of the data model, the translation of metadata in bits of a stream.

---

[101] This paragraph is wholly indebted to, but not literally quoting, the blogpost of Stuart Weibel (2008).

Structure

The syntax needs an unambiguous structure. This is a non-exhaustive list of the things that need to be specified in a well-structured metadata assertion:

- The boundaries of a set of assertions what constitutes a record; what should be described?
- Cardinality - can an element be repeated, and if so, is there a limit on the number?
- How is a name structured? The structure defines and identifies the components, e.g. a name consists of a first and a last name. The 'how' part is defined by the syntax, e.g. the first name is followed by the last name. What is the delimiter, separating elements of a compound name. Many names are compound structures with a surprising and confounding complexity.
- How is nesting managed?
- How are dates encoded? YYYY-MM-DD? DD-MM-YYYY? MM-DD-YYYY?
- How does one identify an encoding scheme that specifies the above question?
- How does one identify a value-encoding scheme, e.g. LCSH, MeSH, Dewey from which metadata values can be chosen? Are such schemes required or optional?
- Are metadata values specified by reference, by URI, or by value, by literal strings?

Protocol

In its simplest form, a protocol can be defined as the rules governing the semantics and syntax, and synchronisation of communication. It enables the communication of the data between two nodes. It is a standard that is very crucial to the repository landscape, such as OAI-PMH.

Defining semantics is a political process of reaching consensus. Syntax is arranging data reliably so they travel in an orderly way between computers and structure is the specification of details necessary to layout and declare metadata assertions so they can be expressed unambiguously in syntax. A data model is the specification of this structure. A protocol enables the connection or communication of data, in a semantic, structured and syntactical way, between two endpoints.

5.1.3 Interoperability in DRIVER II Context

In the DRIVER II project, institutional repositories expose their metadata on freely available publications via Dublin Core[102] XML records on the network. These structured machine-readable records can be harvested via the OAI-PMH protocol[103], indexed, made searchable, disassembled for use in lay-outing of search results, e.g. display only the title and authors, and grouped in citation lists. They can be referenced by their identifier and reasoned about using semantic technologies such as RDF (Resource Desciption Framework)[104]. This is possible because these Dublin Core (DC) records contain the semantics needed for reuse of information, in this case metadata about the publication.

For the publications and their contents themselves, it is not that easy. It is widely agreed that simple DC, as mandated by OAI-PMH, has limitations that pose problems for repository developers and aggregator services. Issues relating to normalised names, use of controlled subject vocabularies or other authority lists, dates and identifiers are common. As an example, for <dc:date> there is nothing to indicate if this is the date of publication or date of modification. It is also problematic to identify full-text. DRIVER gets around this problem by using 'sets'. Simple DC is therefore insufficient to describe scholarly works adequately. Hence the focus of this chapter is on deeper levels of data formats.

Institutional Repositories expose publications using so-called splash pages. These pages contain a description of the publication, its abstract and links to mostly binary PDF files, or audiovisual or raw data files. Although the splash pages are structured (HTML), this information is mostly used for presentation purposes: presenting titles, italics, lists, anchors, not only to the publication but also to library homepages, and next/prev buttons. Even worse, the publications themselves very often are binary files, hence very difficult to access for web crawlers and search engines. Reuse of information as in identification, disassembly, indexing and searchability is not that easily achieved.

On a large scale, extensive system resources are required to extract structured information from millions of pages and binary files.

---

[102] http://dublincore.org (last access on November 23rd, 2008).

[103] http://www.openarchives.org/pmh (last access on November 23rd, 2008).

[104] http://www.w3.org/RDF (last access on November 23rd, 2008).

Processing binary data on this level seems to be feasible only for the biggest players in the field. Because DRIVER II focuses on Enhanced Publications, which contain multiple objects and possibly many kinds of binary files, the issue of data formats and interoperability needs to be considered, in order to make sure the different compound objects remain searchable, indexable and interoperable.

6. Envelopes and Packages

6.1 Introduction

Within digital libraries, there is a need to make a logical whole from the parts that make a publication. A book, for example, can consist of a cover page, chapters and annexes. All these parts form a logical whole for the scholarly publication. Yet, this kind of presentation is orientated around a traditional way of publishing, and represents mostly the structure of the form of the object, not the semantic information of the content (Van de Sompel *et al.*, 2004).

Semantic information can describe the type of relationships between the separate parts. These separate parts can be used for reuse, thus making science more efficient and transparent for improved peer-review. Package and envelope formats can be used to describe and/or contain the complete publication with all its separate parts. In the DRIVER context this is called an Enhanced Publication. An advantage of packaging is that one sees the complete description and objects of the Enhanced Publication in one go, rather than fetching multiple descriptions and objects from other locations.

Foulonneau and André (2008:35) give the following definition of envelopes:

> "XML containers provide a structure to embed multiple metadata records about a resource. They also allow inclusion of the object either by value, e.g. a base64 encoding of the resource, or by reference, e.g. URLs to the different data streams or files that compose the resource."

This section about packages and envelopes contains an introduction and general theory about packages, situated in the DRIVER context of Enhanced Publications. This is followed by different packaging formats, each with their theory and by case studies and outcomes/opportunities for DRIVER. It ends with a concluding comparative table of all the formats described in the foregoing chapter.

6.2 Exchanging packaged Information in the Open Archive Context

For a better understanding of what an envelope or package consists of, the Open Archives Information Systems (OAIS) reference model (Consultative Committee for Space Data Systems, 2002) can be used in order to construct an abstract data-model of an envelope or package, regardless of the standard or technology being used (e.g. DIDL or IMS-CP).

6.2.1 Information Packages

The OAIS reference model introduces the notion of a conceptual container called an *Information Package* (IP), which contains *Information Objects* (IOs).

The OAIS reference model recognises three specialised types of Information Packages:
- Submission Information Package (SIP), used to construct one or more;
- Archival Information Package (AIP);
- Dissemination Information Package (DIP), derived from one or more AIPs.

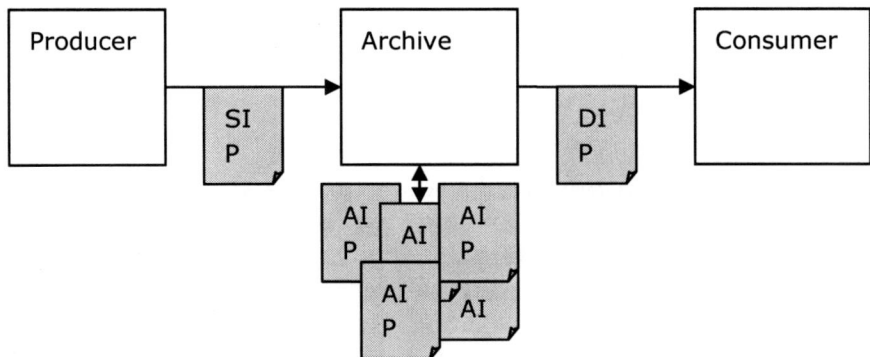

Figure 19. Workflow of Information packages

Figure 19 shows that the SIP is created by a producer or author and handed over to the Archive. The archive can then convert the SIP into an AIP to store the information in an efficient way. To disseminate the information to future users who are interested in the information, the stored information is made available through a DIP. That DIP can be of a format that is useful at that future time for interoperable exchange of information.

6.2.2 Information Objects

An Information Package is a concept that represents a multitude of separate parts (Information Objects) that form a logical whole. These Information Objects consist of Data Objects, e.g. MIME optimised files, and Representation Information, e.g. XML manifest file. The Data Object and Representation Information are in some cases together in a ZIP-file, in other cases they are distributed separately. Figure 20 is inspired on the OAIS model and represents the ideal generic structure of an Information Package.

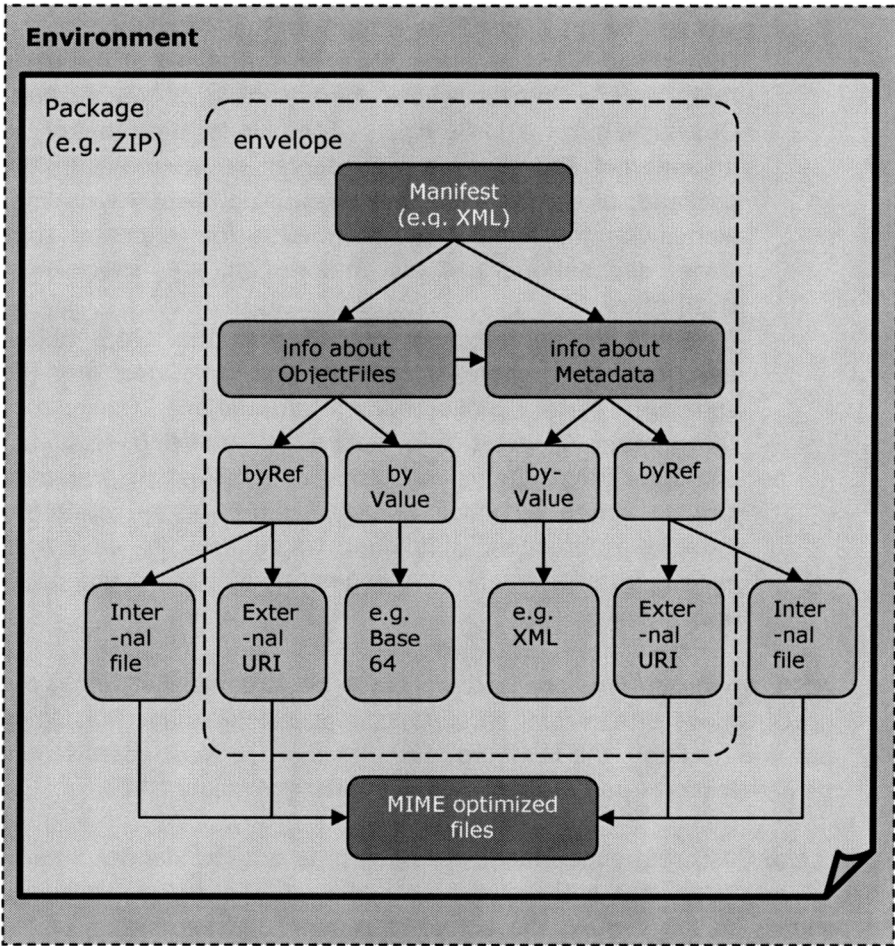

Figure 20. Structure of a generic package in an environment

The terms used in the illustration represent in this context are the following:

- The *Environment* can be a database, file system or web server.

- The *Package* is a compressed file (e.g. ZIP) that contains all files that are part of the whole plus a manifest file. A Package is optional. Files can also exist outside a package on a web server.

- The *Envelope* is a virtual component that represents the manifest file when not in a package.

- The *Manifest* file describes the parts that form a logical whole. These parts can be the ObjectFiles along with the Metadata.
    - *ObjectFiles* in the manifest are representations of the parts that form a logical whole, binary files or ASCII files. ObjectFile information consists of the file location (byRef) to an external source on a web server or internally in the package; or the file itself (byValue) using Base64 encoding; along with the MIME type information for rendering software; and optionally, *Fixity Information,* e.g. checksums, certificates.
    - *Metadata* in the manifest, according to the OAIS model, describes the whole document and can describe the separate parts: Bibliographic Information; Provenance Information; Context Information by asserting relations; Structure Information; and Semantic Information. Metadata can be stored by value in the manifest or by reference. External referencing is pointing to an XML file on a web server. Internal referencing is pointing to a file in the package.

- *MIME optimised files* are uncompressed bit streams that follow the specifications of a certain MIME type, e.g. a JPEG image file. When not in a package, the MIME optimised files are in most cases stored on a web server and are referred to by using absolute URI's.

Using the OAIS reference model, we have been able to identify a number of key elements defining the structure of a package. However, depending on the syntax, the actual placement and expression of the components may vary from the abstract data model. For example, instead of the RI object containing the full specification, it may also contain an identifier such as a MIME-type. Also, the data object may be included by-value, but it may also be included by-reference and identified with an URI.

Although the different object standards discussed below may at first seem incomparable, especially those that use XML containers as an Information Package compared to those that use ZIP archives for that purpose, it is important to note that essentially they are expressing the same abstract data model using different encoding schemas and algorithms, since each of them is able to express the components described above.

Extra Criteria
Five other criteria to create a better understanding of the nature of the package format:
1. Package boundaries specified in specifications;
2. The information that describes the whole and its parts can exist without package boundaries;
3. Extensibility: the specifications allow the XML to be mixed with extended third-party specifications;
4. Forward and backward compatibility;
5. Community type & size.

6.3   The Context of Enhanced Publications

In the DRIVER context there is a need to exchange Enhanced Publications (EP). Woutersen-Windhouwer and Brandsma (2009) gave the following definition:

> "An Enhanced Publication is a publication that is enhanced with research data, extra materials, post publication data, database records, and has an object-based structure with explicit links between the objects. In this definition, an object can be an article or part thereof, a data set, an image, a movie, a comment, a module or a link to information in a database".

So, in this context, three entities must be distinguished: the 'root' publication, other data, and metadata.

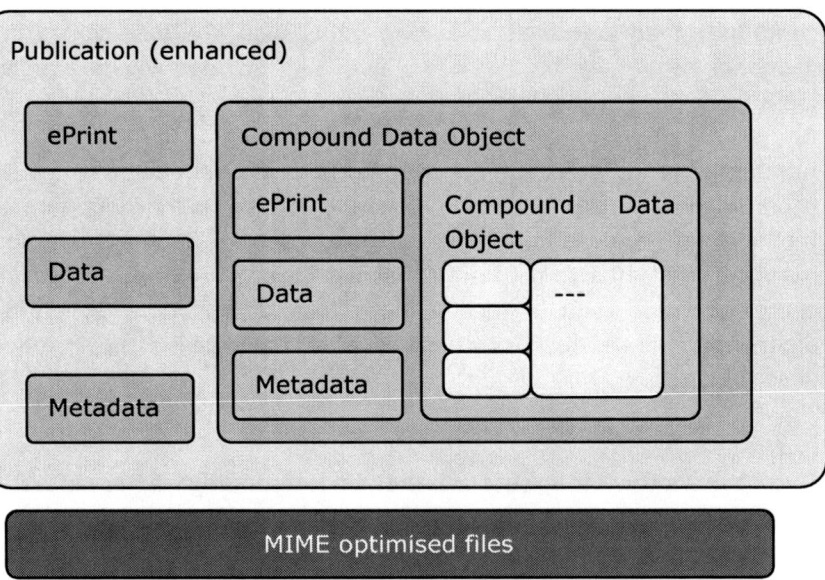

Figure 21. Simple representation of an Enhanced Publication

6.3.1 Criteria for Enhanced Publications

Verhaar (2009) is describing the Object model for Enhanced Publications. This report recommends the following criteria to be reflected in order to create Enhanced Publications:

- It must be possible at any moment to specify the component parts of an Enhanced Publication;
- Enhanced Publications must be available as web resources that can be accessed via a URI. The same goes for their components;
- It must be possible to expand: to add other autonomous compound objects to the publication;
- It must be possible to keep track of the different versions of both the Enhanced Publication as a whole, and of its constituent parts;
- It must be possible to record properties of the resources that are added to the publication, like semantic type, title, author, date modified, mime type, uri;
- It must be possible to record authorship of the Enhanced Publication in its entirety and authorship of its component parts;
- It must be possible to secure the long-term preservation of Enhanced Publications;
- It must be possible to record the relations between the web resources that are part of an Enhanced Publication, like Containment, Sequential, Versioning, Lineage, Manifestations, Bibliographic Citations;

- Institutions that offer access to Enhanced Publications must make sure that they can be discovered;
- Institutions that provide access to Enhanced Publications must ensure that these are available as documents based on the OAI-ORE model.

6.4   MPEG21-DIDL

6.4.1   MPEG-21

For a general definition, Wikipedia describes MPEG-21 as follows:

"The MPEG-21 standard, from the Moving Picture Experts Group aims at defining an open framework for multimedia applications, ISO 21000. ... As an XML-based standard, MPEG-21 is designed to communicate machine-readable license information and do so in a 'ubiquitous, unambiguous and secure' manner. ... MPEG-21 is based on two essential concepts: the definition of a fundamental unit of distribution and transaction, which is the Digital Item, and the concept of users interacting with them. ... Due to that, we could say that the main objective of the MPEG-21 is to define the technology needed to support users to exchange, access, consume, trade or manipulate Digital Items in an efficient and transparent way." [105]

The Multimedia Description Schemes (MDS) Group (2005):

> *"ISO/IEC 21000 defines a set of abstract terms and concepts to form a useful model for declaring Digital Items. The goal of this model is to be as flexible and general as possible, while providing for the 'hooks' that enable higher-level functionality. This, in turn, allows the model to serve as a key foundation in the building of higher-level models in other MPEG-21 elements. This model specifically does not define a language in and of itself. Instead, the model helps to provide a common set of abstract concepts and terms that can be used to define such a scheme, or to perform mappings."*

---

[105] http://en.wikipedia.org/wiki/MPEG-21 (last access on November 23rd, 2008).

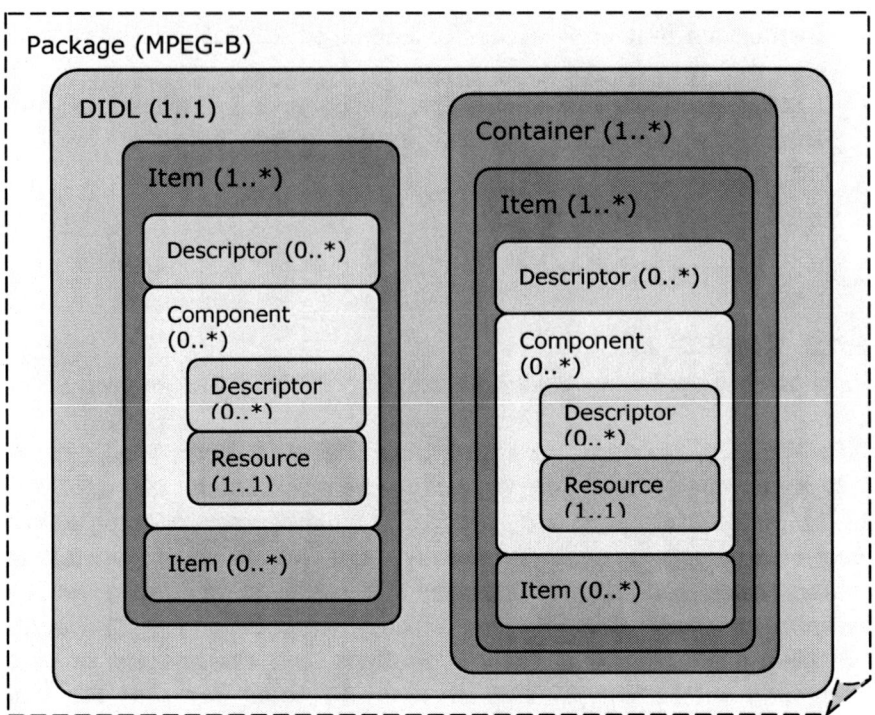

Figure 22. Internal structure of DIDL

6.4.2 DIDL

DIDL (Digital Item Declaration Language) is a subset of the MPEG-21 standard ISO 21000. Declaring a Digital Item involves specifying the resources, metadata, and their interrelationships for a Digital Item. In the library context, again a subset of the available fifteen DIDL elements is used (Bekaert *et al.*, 2003). The DIDL elements can be nested in a particular way. The nested structure of the DIDL Model is provided in Figure 22, with the added cardinalities between brackets. An explanation of the elements is described separately below. With this structure of nested elements a specific scheme can be created for the needs of a community. Practical examples of the use of DIDL can be found in the aDORe project[106] and in the SURFshare Standards wiki[107].

---

[106] http://african.lanl.gov/aDORe/

[107]http://purl.org/REP/standards/MPEG21+DIDL+Application+Profile+for+Institutional+Repositories

- *DIDL*. The DIDL element is the root that describes the boundaries of the DIDL model. Inside this element an Item can be described, or it can contain a container that describes several items.

- *Item*. An item is a grouping of sub-items and/or components that are bound to relevant descriptors. These descriptors contain information about the item. An item that contains no sub-items can be considered a whole. An item that does contain sub-items can be considered a compilation. Items may also contain annotations to their sub-parts.

- *Descriptor*. A descriptor associates information with the enclosing entity. This information may be a component, such as a thumbnail of an image or a text component, or a textual statement. Descriptors may be conditional.

- *Component*. A component is the binding of a resource to a set of descriptors. These descriptors are information concerning all or part of the specific resource instance. A component itself is not an item; components are building blocks of items. Components may be conditional.

- *Resource*. A resource is an individually identifiable Asset such as a video or audio clip, an image, or a textual Asset. A resource may also potentially be a physical object. All resources shall be locatable via an unambiguous address. The resource can contain information by reference, or by value. The value can be for example the metadata encoded in XML, or for example the bit stream encoded by a base64 scheme[108].

MPEG21-DIDL is mainly used in the music and film industry. Only since a few years ago the practical usage for Digital Libraries came into existence with the study from Bekaert *et al.* (2003).

DIDL packaging
In order to package DIDL XML in a compressed archive file, the MPEG specifications demand to use 'Binary MPEG format for XML' also referred

---

[108] Base64: encodes binary data by treating it numerically and translating it into a base 64 representation, http://en.wikipedia.org/wiki/Base64 (last access on November 23rd, 2008).

to as BiM or MPEG-B[109]. MPEG-B is an optimised encoding scheme for XML structures, to stream large XML files over the Internet.

6.4.3 Case Studies

In the case of Digital Libraries, five communities in the US and in Europe have adopted MPEG21-DIDL to their repositories:

- The aDORe project in Los Alamos Digital Library;
- the DARE programme in the Netherlands;
- the NEEO project[110] for European Economists where over 50.000 documents are exchanged for creating the EconomistsOnline portal[111];
- the University of Ghent adopted DIDL for their topographic collection[112];
- Fedora commons[113] with a big user community.

In the Los Alamos National Laboratory Digital Library alone, 5 million DIDL records exist. In the Netherlands, 14 Dutch repositories create DIDL records on demand of an OAI-PMH request; the amount of Open Access materials was over 150.000 records in July 2008.

In the case of the Dutch repositories, DIDL is extensively used to build services from the data it is withholding as a compound object. Three service providers harvest this material:

- *The NARCIS portal*[114]. This portal, successor of the former DAREnet[115], collects all scientific information in the Netherlands and makes it freely accessible.

---

[109] ISO/IEC 21000-9, Information technology — Multimedia framework (MPEG-21) — Part 9: File Format.
http://www.iso.org/iso/iso_catalogue/catalogue_tc/catalogue_detail.htm?csnumber=40639 (last access on November 23rd, 2008).
[110] NEEO, Network of European Economists Online; for further information see:
http://www.nereus4economics.info/neeo_intro_press.html (last access on November 23rd, 2008).
[111] For a pilot of the EconomistsOnline search facility, see:
http://publications.uvt.nl/eo/index.html (last access on November 23rd, 2008).
[112] http://adore.ugent.be/topo/?language=en (last access on December 8th, 2008).
[113] http://fedora-commons.org/ (last access on December 4th, 2003).
[114] http://www.narcis.info/index (last access on November 23rd, 2008).

- *The National Resolution Service.* This service makes it able to resolve persistent identifiers by redirecting to the splash page.

- *The e-Depot.* This service is provided by the Dutch National Library, which collects national scientific outputs for Long Term Preservation purposes.

The use of DIDL originates out of the SURFshare programme[116], which followed up on the DARE programme. The aim of the SURFshare programme is to establish a joint infrastructure that advances the accessibility as well as the exchange of scientific information. From this point of view, DIDL is used in repositories that expose Open Access publications along with the links to the full-text documents, the metadata, the persistent identifier that refers to the publication as a whole and the splash page of the publication at the side of the local repository. In Table 8 an example is given of the SURFshare DIDL structure where it is possible to describe the whole and the separate parts, as well as the relations and the semantic types.

```
<didl:DIDL> <!-- Introducing the DIDL document.  -->
   <didl:Item>  <!-- The Item is the autonomous entity that
represents the whole work-->
      <!-- now follow the sub-Items that describe the parts,
metadata, object files and splash page -->

      <didl:Item> <!-- Introducing the area for OAI_DC metadata  -->
         <didl:Descriptor> <!-- ObjectType of Item -->
         <didl:Statement mimeType="application/xml">
            <dip:ObjectType>info:eu-
repo/semantics/descriptiveMetadata</dip:ObjectType>
         </didl:Statement>
         </didl:Descriptor>
         <didl:Component> <!-- Actual resource of Item -->
         <didl:Resource mimeType="application/xml">
            <oai_dc:dc>
               <dc:title>Neonatal Glucocorticoid Treatment
...</dc:title>
               <dc:creator>Bal, M.P.</dc:creator>
            </oai_dc:dc>
         </didl:Resource>
         </didl:Component>
      </didl:Item>
```

---

[115] http://www.narcis.info/index/tab/darenet (last access on November 23rd, 2008).

[116] Further information on the SURFShare programma and about the DIDL application can be found at
http://www.surffoundation.nl/smartsite.dws?id=5289&ch=ENG (last access on November 23rd, 2008).

```
    <didl:Item> <!-- Introducing the intermediate page -->
        <didl:Descriptor> <!-- ObjectType of Item -->
            <didl:Statement mimeType="application/xml">
                <dip:ObjectType>info:eu-
repo/semantics/humanStartPage</dip:ObjectType>
            </didl:Statement>
        </didl:Descriptor>
        <didl:Component> <!-- Actual resource of Item -->
            <didl:Resource mimeType="text/html"
                ref="http://igitur-
archive.library.uu.nl/dissertations/2006-1206-200250/UUindex.html"/>
        </didl:Component>
    </didl:Item>

    <!-- Introducing the area for digital fulltext objects -->

    <didl:Item> <!--Bitstream no: [0] -->
        <didl:Descriptor> <!-- ObjectType of Item -->
            <didl:Statement mimeType="application/xml">
                <dip:ObjectType>info:eu-
repo/semantics/objectFile</dip:ObjectType>
            </didl:Statement>
        </didl:Descriptor>
        <didl:Component> <!-- Actual resource of Item -->
            <didl:Resource mimeType="text/html"

    ref="https://dspace.library.uu.nl:8443/bitstream/18/index.htm"/>
        </didl:Component>
    </didl:Item>

    <didl:Item> <!--Bitstream no: [1] -->
        <didl:Descriptor> <!-- ObjectType of Item -->
            <didl:Statement mimeType="application/xml">
                <dip:ObjectType>info:eu-
repo/semantics/objectFile</dip:ObjectType>
            </didl:Statement>
        </didl:Descriptor>
        <didl:Component> <!-- Actual resource of Item -->
            <didl:Resource mimeType="image/jpeg"
    ref=https://dspace.library.uu.nl:8443/bitstream/1874/15290/16/bal
.jpg/>
        </didl:Component>
    </didl:Item>
    </didl:Item>
</didl:DIDL>
```

Table 8. Example of the SURFshare DIDL structure.

6.4.4 Opportunities for DRIVER

Due to the generic framework of DIDL, it is possible to implement it in multiple contexts. One can shape DIDL into an application profile that is suitable for a specific community. Machines can still read and interpret the data in DIDL. Scholarly communication models that will be used in the future will probably fit in DIDL, e.g. when a publication is not based on paper, but on video for example.

DIDL can be extended easily with semantics and OAI-ORE attributes and elements, which makes DIDL useful for expressing Enhanced Publications.

6.5 METS

6.5.1 Theory of METS

METS stands for 'Metadata Encoding and Transmission Standard' and has been created by the Library of Congress of the United States[117]. METS is a data encoding and transmission specification, expressed in XML, that provides the means to convey the metadata necessary for both the management of digital objects within a repository and the exchange of such objects between repositories or between repositories and their users.

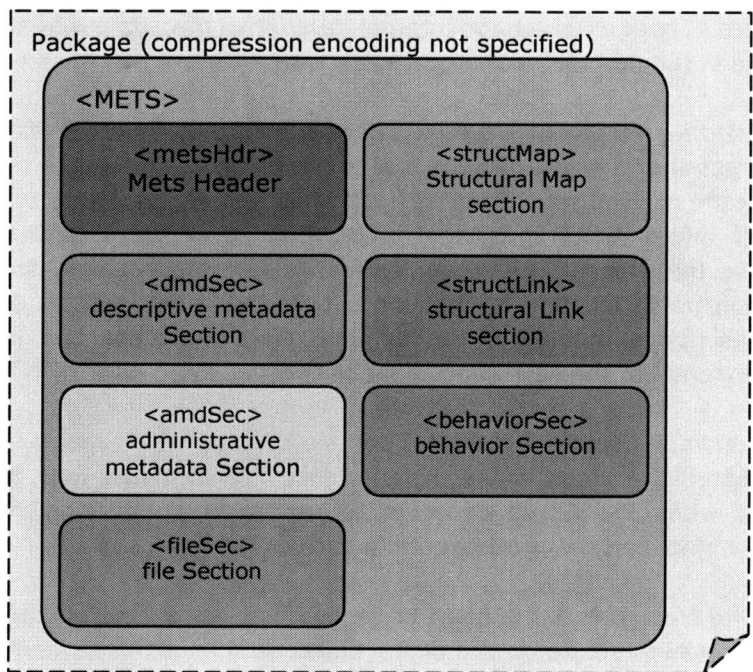

Figure 23. The internal structure of the METS format

This common object format was designed to allow the sharing of efforts to develop information management tools/services and to facilitate the

---

[117] http://www.loc.gov/standards/mets (last access on November 23rd, 2008).

interoperable exchange of digital materials among institutions, including vendors.

The METS document structure consists of seven major sections, which may contain a variety of elements and attributes as specified in the METS schema. At the most general level, a METS document may contain the following sections:

- *METS Header.* The METS Header contains metadata describing the METS document itself, including such information as creator and editor.

- *Descriptive Metadata Section.* This section contains descriptive metadata that is external to the METS document, e.g. a MARC record in an OPAC or a MODS record maintained on a WWW server, internally embedded descriptive metadata, or both. Multiple instances of both external and internal descriptive metadata may be included in the descriptive metadata section.

- *Administrative Metadata Section.* Information about how the files were created and stored, intellectual property rights, metadata regarding the original source object from which the digital object was derived, information regarding the provenance of the files that comprise the object, i.e. master/derivative file relationships, and migration/transformation information is collected in this section. As with descriptive metadata, the administrative metadata can be either external to the METS document or encoded internally.

- *File Section.* A list of all files that contain content which make up the electronic versions of the digital object. File elements may be grouped within File Group elements, to provide for subdividing the files by object version or other criteria such as file type, size.

- *Structural Map.* This is the heart of the METS document. It outlines a hierarchical structure for the digital object, and links the elements of that structure to content files and metadata that pertain to each element. The structural map is the only mandatory section in a METS document.

- *Structural Links.* Allows the creator of the METS document to record the existence of hyperlinks between nodes in the hierarchy outlined in the Structural Map. This is of particular value in using METS to archive Websites or other hypermedia.

- *Behaviour Section.* A behaviour section can be used to associate executable behaviours with the content of the object encoded using METS. Each behaviour element within a behaviour section has an interface definition element that represents an abstract definition of behaviours represented by a particular behaviour section. Each behaviour element also has a mechanism element that identifies a module of executable code that implements and runs the behaviours defined by the interface definition.

6.5.2 Case Studies

METS is very well known in the Library and Archive world, where the standard is used as an Archival Information Package for Long Term Preservation storage. The Library of Congress registers the contributed application profiles of communities across the globe of National Libraries and Universities[118].

METS has also penetrated the market of DSpace and Fedora Commons repository software where software developers have implemented METS into this software for native support on ingestion and export. METS is used as a Dissemination Information Package in the DIAS system, developed by IBM and in use by the National Libraries in the Netherlands and in Germany (Verhoeven, 2006), also OCLC's Digital Archive disseminates METS records (Surface, 2003). In Table 9 an example is provided that shows the XML structure of a METS package used by the Oxford Digital Library.

```
<mets:mets>
  <mets:metsHdr RECORDSTATUS="interim"/> <!-- Header Section -->

  <mets:dmdSec ID="munahi010-aag-dmd-0001"> <!-- Descriptive
Metadata Section -->
    <mets:mdWrap LABEL="MODS Metadata" MDTYPE="MODS"
MIMETYPE="text/xml">
      <mets:xmlData>
        <mods:mods>
          <mods:titleInfo>
            <mods:title>A Catalogue of the Organic...</mods:title>
          </mods:titleInfo>
        </mods:mods>
```

---

[118] http://www.loc.gov/standards/mets/mets-registered-profiles.html (last access on November 23rd, 2008).

```
        </mets:xmlData>
      </mets:mdWrap>
    </mets:dmdSec>

    <mets:amdSec ID="munahi010-aag-amd-0001"> <!--Administrative
Metadata Section -->
      <mets:techMD ID="munahi010-aag-tmd-0001-0">
        <mets:mdRef LOCTYPE="URL" MDTYPE="OTHER"
xlink:href="file:/munahi010-aag-0001-0.xml"/>
      </mets:techMD>
    </mets:amdSec>

    <mets:fileSec> <!-- File Section -->
      <mets:fileGrp ID="munahi010-aag-fgrp-0001">
        <mets:file ADMID="munahi010-aag-tmd-0001-0" ID="munahi010-aag-
0001-0" MIMETYPE="image/tiff">
          <mets:FLocat LOCTYPE="URL"
xlink:href="file://hfs.ox.ac.uk/munahi010-aag-0001.tiff"/>
        </mets:file>
      </mets:fileGrp>
    </mets:fileSec>

    <mets:structMap> <!--Structural Map Section -->
      <mets:div ID="munahi010-aag-div.1" LABEL="Short Title">
        <mets:div ID="munahi010-aag-div.1.1" LABEL="Half Title Page">
          <mets:fptr FILEID="munahi010-aag-fgrp-0001"/>
        </mets:div>
      </mets:div>
    </mets:structMap>

</mets:mets>
```

Table 9. Simple example of METS XML, used by the Oxford Digital Library[119]

6.5.3   Opportunities for DRIVER

METS is used for representing the logical structure of traditional digital publications. Therefore, according to the METS specifications, the publication is only described as a whole, on package level, and not for the separate parts. Natively, the separate parts are only described by a MimeType and a Label. The format can be extended by community-specific application profiles to provide support of descriptive metadata for the separate parts. With such extensions, it is possible to create Enhanced Publications where the separate parts can be easily reused, which is a good feature for DRIVER.

---

[119] Oxford Digital Library METS example:

http://www.loc.gov/standards/mets/examples-profiles/sample1.xml (last access on November 23rd, 2008).

6.6 IMS Content Package

6.6.1 Theory of IMS-CP

The IMS Content Package (IMS-CP), current version 1.1.4, dating from October 2004, is the de facto standard for packaging educational or learning content for transport across Learning Management Systems (LMSs) and Virtual Learning Environments (VLEs).

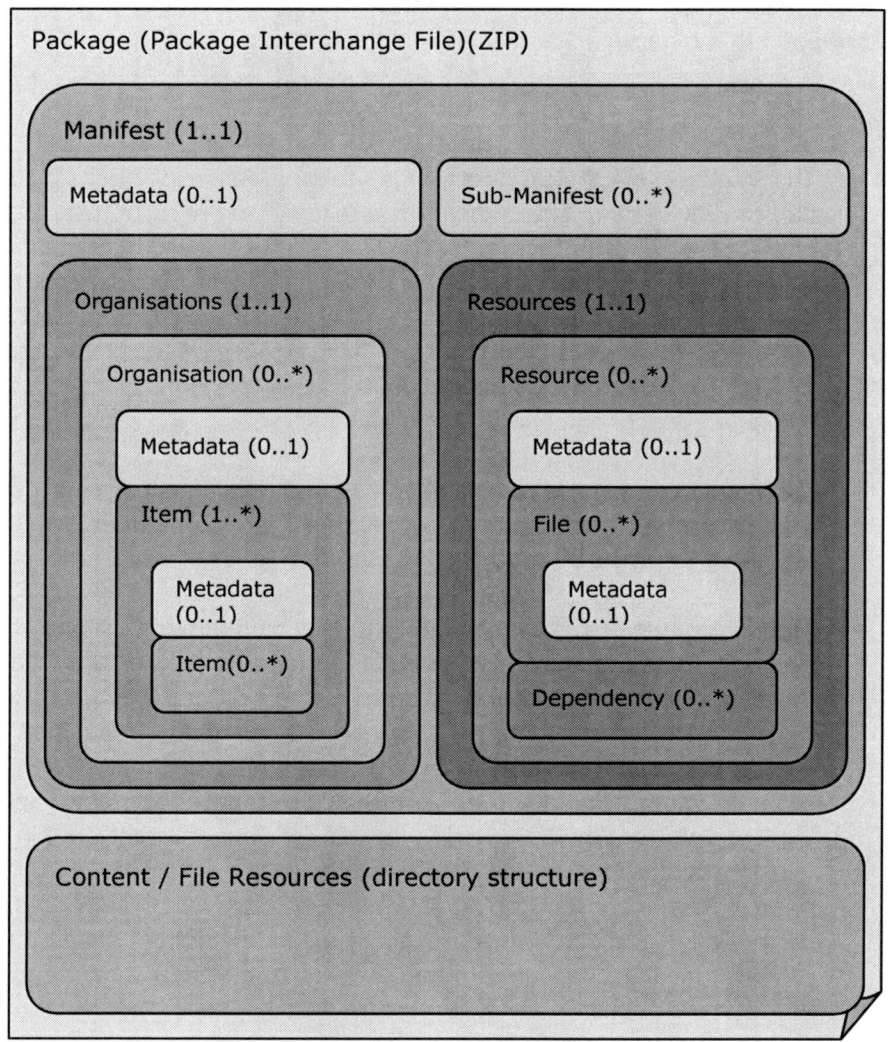

Figure 24. IMS package with content part and manifest XML structure

The purpose of the IMS Content framework is to enable the encapsulation of all the content resources in a concise and easy-to-browse manner. It supports the information and structure required to promote interoperable online learning experiences. The information model of the IMS-CP, as depicted in Figure 24, consists of three key elements, the content, the manifest file and the package. The actual files placed in a directory structure form the content, the manifest file describes the content. Both the directory structure and manifest file are wrapped in a binary package as a single compressed file.

The IMS Content Framework consists of the following elements:

- The *Package* is a logical directory containing a specially named XML file, any XML control documents it directly references (e.g. an XSD or DTD file) and the actual file resources. These resources may be organised in sub-directories. A Package has a clear boundary for the context in which it can be interpreted. This boundary can be a CD-ROM or a single ZIP file that conforms to RFC 1951 (Deutsch, 1996). The ZIP file can be distributed and therefore is called the Package Interchange File (PIF).

- *File Resources.* These are the actual media elements, text files, graphics, and other resources as described by the manifest(s). The file resources may be organised in sub-directories.

- *Top-level Manifest.* A mandatory XML element describing the Package itself. It may also contain optional sub-Manifests. Each instance of a manifest contains the following sections:
  - *Meta-data* section. An XML element describing a manifest as a whole;
  - *Organisations* section. An XML element describing zero, one, or multiple organisations of the content within a manifest;
  - *Resources* section. An XML element containing references to all of the actual resources and media elements needed for a manifest, including meta-data describing the resources, and references to any external files;
  - *sub-Manifest.* One or more optional, logically nested manifests.

Version Differences between IMS-CP and LOM

The IMS-CP is usually implemented with the metadata-set defined in IMS-Learning Resource Meta-Data (IMSMD) specification v1.2.1 or IEEE 1484.12.3 standard for XML Schema binding for Learning Object Metadata (LOM) defined in IEEE 1484.12.1.

Although some discrepancies used to exist between IMSMD and IEEE-LOM across the various versions, as of IMSMD version 1.3, the specifications have been realigned with IEEE 1484.12.1 and IEEE 1484.12.3. Changes include both vocabulary and serialisation, the latter one mainly translating itself into a different use of attributes in the XML.

6.6.2 Case Study LOREnet

IMS-CP is extensively used in the educational field to distribute Learning Objects. The IMS-Content Package is not only used by publishers of Learning Objects, but also in virtual learning environments such as Blackboard and WebCT. Also, application profiles have been created to match community specific needs, like extensions for courses in SCORM and Dutch vocabularies in LOREnet[120]. LOREnet is a Dutch search portal for learning objects. This portal harvests via the OAI-PMH protocol Learning Object Metadata (LOM) from repositories.

IEEE-LOM Informational Model

The IEEE-LOM informational model describes 58 elements grouped into nine chapters:
1. General;
2. Lifecycle;
3. Metametadata;
4. Technical;
5. Educational;
6. Rights;
7. Relation;
8. Annotation, and
9. Classification.

Within the technical chapter of the LOM metadata the location to the learning object is specified. This can be an IMS Content Package (ZIPfile) or a bit stream to the digital learning object. LOREnet makes it possible to download content packages and reuse them in, for example,

---

[120] http://www.lorenet.nl/en/page/luzi/show?name=show&showcase=1 (last access on November 23rd, 2008): LOREnet Learning Object Portal.

an Electronic Learning Environment such as Blackboard or WebCT. If no content package is available at the repository, LOREnet simply creates one on the fly.

In Table 10, a simplified version of an IMS manifest XML file is shown. This manifest file is created on the fly by LOREnet. Along with the manifest file, a file called "Wat_is_entropie.asf" is placed in the same directory of the Package. The OAI-PMH interface of LOREnet offers IMS Content packages by exposing LORE-LOM. This makes it possible to reuse the content for other service providers in a standard way.

```
<manifest>
  <metadata>
    <lom xmlns="http://ltsc.ieee.org/xsd/LOM">
      <general>
        <title>
          <string language="nl">Wat is entropie?</string>
          <string language="en">What is entropy?</string>
        </title>
        <language>en</language>
        <description>
          <string language="en">An introduction to the concept of
entropy. First, different forms of energy and the laws of
thermodynamics are discussed. Then, examples are examined from the
fields of physics, chemistry and biology. Finally, entropy is shown
to be closely connected to the concept of evolution</string>
        </description>
      </general>
      <lifeCycle>
      <metaMetadata>
        <metadataSchema>LORENET</metadataSchema>
      </metaMetadata>
      <technical>
        <format>video/x-ms-wmv</format>

<location>http://streamingmedia.uva.nl/playlist/windowsmedia/64E5597
E-0D6B-B90F-73AC-
D264D704945C_/IIS_Karel_van_Dam_Entropie_normalised.asx</location>
      </technical>
      <educational/>
      <rights/>
      <classification/>
    <lom/>
  </metadata>
  <organisations/>
  <resources>
    <resource identifier="ref1" type="webcontent"
href="Wat_is_entropie.asf">
      <metadata/>
      <file href="Wat_is_entropie.asf" />
    </resource>
  </resources>
</manifest>
```

Table 10. Simplified example of IMS-CP manifest file with LORE-LOM

6.6.3 Opportunities for DRIVER

The DRIVER infrastructure can harvest and create content packages as single ZIP files. These packages are authored in a specific context where the actual data is separated from a repository and can exist as an entity by itself on local hard disks, where it can be spread and reused.

The major advantage of the IMS-CP manifest for DRIVER, is that it defines a structure where files can be linked to metadata, even if the structure is nested.

6.7 ODF Packages

6.7.1 Theory

The Open Document Format is an open, XML-based file format for office applications, ISO 26300:2006. The OpenDocument format uses a package concept to wrap content and separate files into a single compressed file. Separate files may be media files used in an ODF document like images, audio, and video. ODF is also mentioned in Paragraph 4.2.8, in parallel with OOXML. Both ODF and OOXML can be described from a package perspective as well as from a mark-up perspective.

Method

The ODF specifications state the following about their package method:

> *"OpenDocument uses a package file to store the XML content of a document together with its associated binary data, and to optionally compress the XML content. This package is a standard ZIP file, whose structure is discussed below. Information about the files contained in the package is stored in an XML file called the manifest file. The manifest file is always stored at the pathname META-INF/manifest.xml. The main pieces of information stored in the manifest are a list of all of the files in the package and the media type of each file in the package. If a file stored in the package is encrypted, decryption information required to decrypt the file is stored in the manifest"* (Durusau et al., 2007: 709).

Internal Structure

The internal structure of the ODF package is shown in Figure 25. This package contains a manifest file that describes all the files inside the package including the metadata file, styles, content and settings by using the file-entry element. In this element, attributes of the media-type and full-path to the file within the package are presented. Optionally, there is an attribute for the uncompressed file size when the file is encrypted. Encryption-data is provided for the file-entry to decrypt the file.

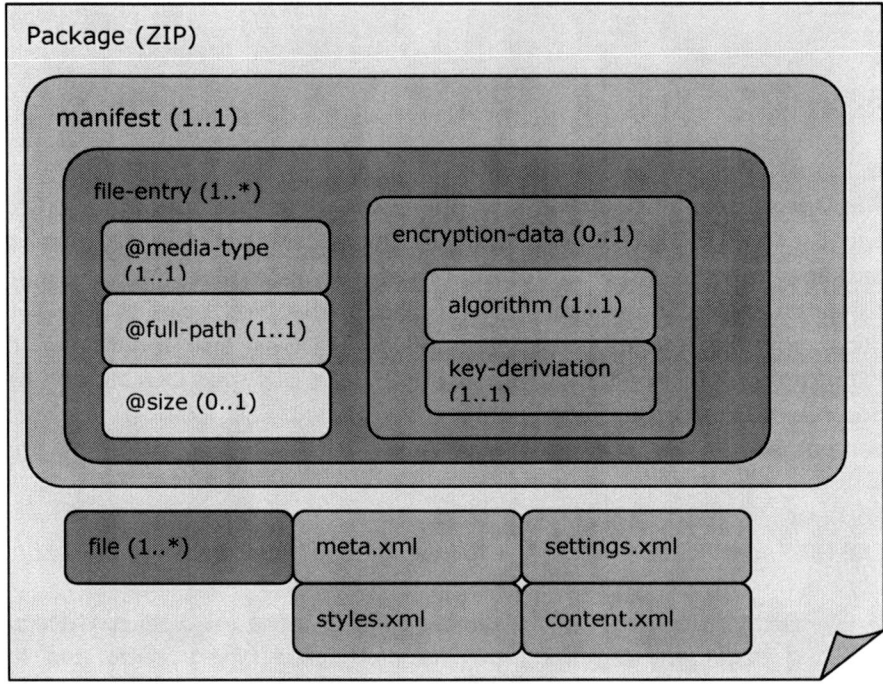

Figure 25. The internal structure of an ODF package

6.7.2 Case Studies

The Open Document Format is being used, implemented and supported by a large community. ODF is used in software like the Open Office Suite and Content Management System 'Alfresco'. The European Union supports the use of ODF.

```
<manifest:manifest

xmlns:manifest="urn:oasis:names:tc:opendocument:xmlns:manifest:1.0">
    <manifest:file-entry
        manifest:media-type="application/vnd.oasis.opendocument.text"
        manifest:full-path="/"/>
    <manifest:file-entry manifest:media-type="image/jpeg"
        manifest:full-
path="Pictures/10000000000003200000258912EB1C3.jpg"
        manifest:size="66704">
            <manifest:encryption-data>
            <manifest:algorithm manifest:algorithm-name="Blowfish CFB"
            manifest:initialisation-vector="T+miu403484="/>
                <manifest:key-derivation manifest:key-derivation-
name="PBKDF2"
                manifest:iteration-count="1024"
                manifest:salt="aNYdmqv4cObAJSJjm4RzqA=="/>
            </manifest:encryption-data>
    </manifest:file-entry>
    <manifest:file-entry
        manifest:media-type="text/xml" manifest:full-
path="content.xml"
        manifest:size="3143">
        <manifest:encryption-data>
            <manifest:algorithm manifest:algorithm-name="Blowfish CFB"
                manifest:initialisation-vector="T+miu403484="/>
                <manifest:key-derivation manifest:key-derivation-
name="PBKDF2"
                manifest:iteration-count="1024"
                manifest:salt="aNYdmqv4cObAJSJjm4RzqA=="/>
        </manifest:encryption-data>
    </manifest:file-entry>
    <manifest:file-entry
            manifest:media-type="text/xml" manifest:full-
path="meta.xml"/>
</manifest:manifest>
```

Table 11. Simplified XML example of the ODF package manifest file

In Table 11 a simplified example of a simple Open Document text file is found. It consists of the text document (content.xml), a picture (.jpeg) and the metadata (meta.xml).

ODF is in use in the Open Office applications currently available. The ODF package clearly defines the basic information of the separate files to describe a whole. The information provided in the manifest file is basic enough for an application to open a file. The metadata file in ODF provides information about the whole, not about the separate parts. This makes it perhaps harder to use in scholarly communication. Still, ODF is a widely used and supported ISO standard, and it would be interesting to discover the possibility of adding ORE-semantics to this model.

6.7.3 Opportunities for DRIVER

According to the ODF specifications, only MIME type information is supported. This is a disadvantage of ODF. However, ODF could be easily extended to support Enhanced Publications. By extending the file-entry element with relations and semantics, ODF could support re-usable Enhanced Publications. The large eco-system of ODF, as well as its applicability for many users and its openness, makes it also an interesting standard to follow.

6.8   OOXML Open Package Convention

6.8.1   Theory

Office Open XML file format (OOXML), published in November 2008 as an ISO standard (ISO/IEC 29500:2008)[121], is a standard for word-processing documents, presentations, charts and spreadsheets that is intended to be implemented by multiple applications on multiple platforms. One of its objectives is to ensure the long-term preservation of documents created over the last two decades using programmes that are becoming incompatible with continuing advances in the field of information technology.

ISO/IEC 29500:2008[122] consists of the following four parts:

- ISO/IEC 29500-1:2008, Information technology. Document description and processing languages – Office Open XML File Formats – Part 1: Fundamentals and Markup Language Reference (5 570 pages). This defines a set of XML vocabularies for representing word-processing documents, spreadsheets and presentations.

---

[121] Standard ISO/IEC 29500:2008 is publicly available from:
http://standards.iso.org/ittf/PubliclyAvailableStandards/index.html (last access on December 1st, 2008).

[122] The information in this bullet list is taken from the press release:
http://www.iso.org/iso/pressrelease.htm?refid=Ref1181 (last access on December 5th, 2008).

However, it should be noted that the references to MS Office 2008 in this press release were errors, and have therefore been omitted. This was confirmed in a personal email from Doug Mahugh (Senior Program Manager, Office Interoperability, Microsoft) on 8/12/08.

- *ISO/IEC 29500-2:2008, Information technology.* Document description and processing languages – Office Open XML File Formats – Part 2: Open Packaging Conventions (138 pages). This defines a general-purpose file/component packaging facility, which is built on top of the widely used ZIP file structure. The OPC is described in this paragraph.

- *ISO/IEC 29500-3:2008, Information technology.* Document description and processing languages – Office Open XML File Formats – Part 3: Markup Compatibility and Extensibility (46 pages). This defines a general-purpose mechanism to extend an XML vocabulary.

- *ISO/IEC 29500-4:2008, Information technology.* Document description and processing languages – Office Open XML File Formats – Part 4: Transitional Migration Features (1 475 pages). This defines a set of XML elements and attributes, over and above those defined by ISO/IEC 29500-1, that provide support for legacy Microsoft Office applications.

Office 2007 currently supports the earlier ECMA version of the OOXML standard[123] (ECMA-376). Support for the ISO version (ISO/IEC 29500:2008) will not be implemented until Office 14. An Office Open XML document file contains mainly XML based files compressed within a ZIP package. It also contains binary files for images, video and audio that can be embedded in the Office Document, this according to the Open Package Convention[124].

The OPC defines the structure of the document by the following three components:

- *Content Type* identifies the type of content that is stored in the source part. Content types define a media type, a subtype, and an optional set of parameters.

---

[123] http://www.ecma-international.org/publications/standards/Ecma-376.htm (last access on Dec 11th, 2008).
[124] Open package Convention on Wikipedia:
http://en.wikipedia.org/wiki/Open_Packaging_Convention (last access on December 1st, 2008).

- *Relationship* represents the type of connection between a source part and a target resource. The relationship component makes the connection directly discoverable without looking at the content part, so the relationship is independent of content-specific schemas and quickly to resolve. The Relationship type is a URI that defines the role of the relationship.

- *Digital Signature* contains information to validate the content.

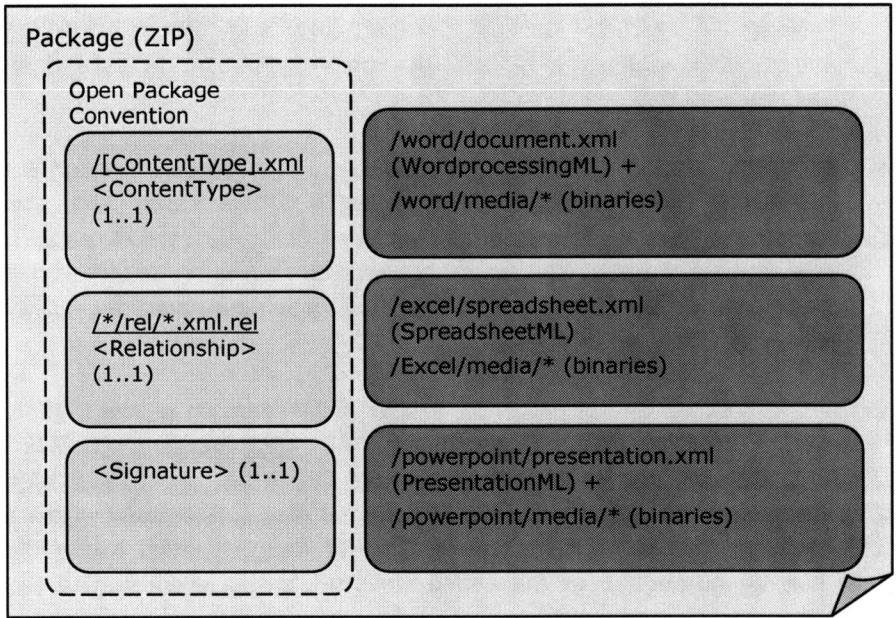

Figure 26. Components used to create an OOXML file.

A technical detail in the OPC is that the relationship structure could allow one to relate metadata files to each separate part. The custom XML component enables it to include other XML data, for example another metadata format.

6.8.2 Case Studies OOXML Open Package Convention
OOXML is introduced with the MS Office Suite 2007. It is expected the market share of the new Office suite will continue to grow. A great deal of consumers and businesses will be using this new format. The number of this format is enormous and in reach of use by a variety of people, including scientists and researchers.

The OOXML format is very complex and the XML files and binary files are distributed in various directories within the ZIP-file. The table below shows the [Content].xml file of a MSWord2007 document that contains some text and an image. This file tells what kind of content the office application can expect to find in the ZIP-file.

```
<Types
xmlns="http://schemas.openxmlformats.org/package/2006/content-
types">
    <Default Extension="png" ContentType="image/png"/>
    <Override PartName="/customXml/itemProps2.xml"
        ContentType="application/vnd.openxmlformats-
officedocument.customXmlProperties+xml"/>
    <Override PartName="/customXml/itemProps3.xml"
        ContentType="application/vnd.openxmlformats-
officedocument.customXmlProperties+xml"/>
    <Override PartName="/customXml/itemProps1.xml"
        ContentType="application/vnd.openxmlformats-
officedocument.customXmlProperties+xml"/>
    <Default Extension="rels"
ContentType="application/vnd.openxmlformats-
package.relationships+xml"/>
    <Default Extension="xml" ContentType="application/xml"/>
    <Override PartName="/word/document.xml"
        ContentType="application/vnd.openxmlformats-
officedocument.wordprocessingml.document.main+xml"/>
    <Override PartName="/word/styles.xml"
        ContentType="application/vnd.openxmlformats-
officedocument.wordprocessingml.styles+xml"/>
    <Override PartName="/docProps/app.xml"
        ContentType="application/vnd.openxmlformats-
officedocument.extended-properties+xml"/>
    <Override PartName="/word/settings.xml"
        ContentType="application/vnd.openxmlformats-
officedocument.wordprocessingml.settings+xml"/>
    <Override PartName="/docProps/custom.xml"
        ContentType="application/vnd.openxmlformats-
officedocument.custom-properties+xml"/>
    <Override PartName="/word/theme/theme1.xml"
        ContentType="application/vnd.openxmlformats-
officedocument.theme+xml"/>
    <Override PartName="/word/fontTable.xml"
        ContentType="application/vnd.openxmlformats-
officedocument.wordprocessingml.fontTable+xml"/>
    <Override PartName="/word/webSettings.xml"
        ContentType="application/vnd.openxmlformats-
officedocument.wordprocessingml.webSettings+xml"/>
    <Override PartName="/docProps/core.xml"
        ContentType="application/vnd.openxmlformats-package.core-
properties+xml"/>
</Types>
```

Table 12. Simple example of OOXML [ContentType].xml , a text with an image.

6.8.3 Opportunities for DRIVER

There has been considerable controversy on the development of OOXML (Ditch, 2007). First is the issue that Microsoft chose not to support the existing international standard (ODF). The ODF Alliance UK Action Group claims that two competing standards are against the very concept of a standard[125]. Secondly, there were many concerns about the rushed management process for approval of OOXML. South Africa, Brazil, India, Denmark and Venezuela lodged appeals against the decision to approve, claiming that the voting process was marred by irregularities. Thirdly, the quality of the specification document has been questioned.

This report will not go into the further details of this discussion, but wishes to treat ODF and OOXML in parallel, yet separately. Both have their advantages and disadvantages for DRIVER. The Office Open XML standard was deemed important for this interoperability chapter because many research publications in repositories originate from MS Office formats and need to stay accessible and compatible. MS Office tools with OOXML will also support the creation of Enhanced Publications; hence the researcher does not need to change environments for creating EP's. This interoperability is one of the advantages of OOXML and the reason why this is considered as an important standard for DRIVER.

Nevertheless, there is a lot of ongoing criticism of OOXML[126], which is a risk factor for adopting the standard. Also, the EU does not recommend the use of closed software: although OOXML is an open specification, it is still very much tied to the closed software that MS Office is.

6.9   Open eBook Package

6.9.1   Theory

Open eBook formats are created and maintained by the International Digital Publishing Forum (IDPF). IDPF is the trade and standards association for the digital publishing industry. The eBook format has three components: the Open Publication Structure (OPS), Open Packaging Format (OPF) and Open Container Format (OCF).

---

[125] http://en.wikipedia.org/wiki/Ooxml (last access on November 24th, 2008).

[126] See, for example: http://www.noooxml.org/ , last access on December 3rd, 2008.

142

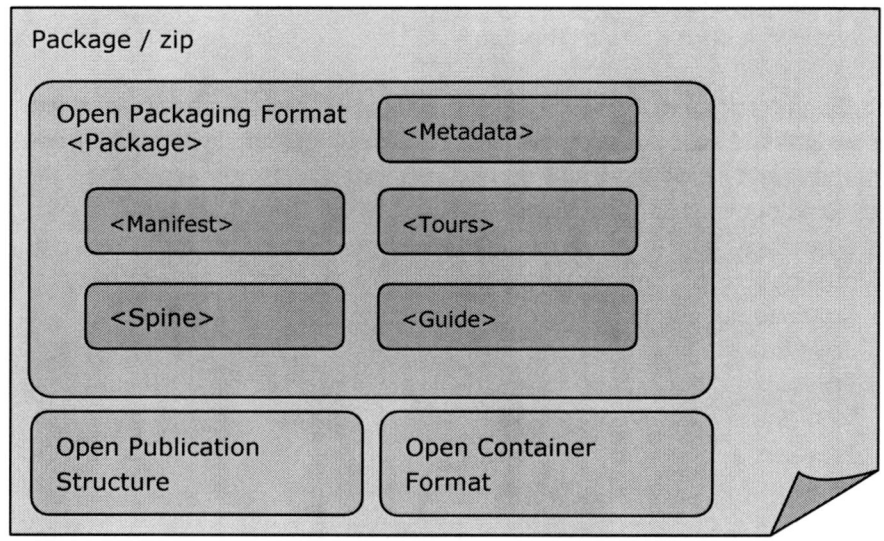

Figure 27. Structure of the Open eBook package Format (OPF)

Format

OPF describes the different elements as follows in the <Package>:

- <Metadata> The required metadata element is used to provide information about the publication as a whole;
- <Manifest> The required manifest provides a list of all the files, or item elements, that are parts of the publication, e.g. Content Documents, style sheets, image files, any embedded font files, any included schemas. The order of item elements in the manifest is not important;
- <Spine> This element defines the reading order of the publication. There is one spine element, which contains one or more itemref elements. Each itemref references an OPS Content Document designated in the manifest;
- <Tours> As much as a tour-guide might assemble points of interest into a set of sightseers' tours, a content provider could assemble selected parts of a publication into a set of tours to enable convenient navigation;
- <Guides> The guide element identifies fundamental structural components of the publication, to enable Reading Systems to provide convenient access to them. The structural components of the books are listed in reference elements contained within the guide element. These components could refer to the table of

contents, list of illustrations, foreword, bibliography, and many other standard parts of the book.

The Open Packaging Format (OPF) specification defines the mechanism by which the various components of an OPS publication are tied together and provides additional structure and semantics to the electronic publication, specifically OPF[127]:

- Describes and references all components of the electronic publication, e.g. markup files, images, navigation structures;
- Provides publication-level metadata;
- Specifies the linear reading-order of the publication;
- Provides fallback information to use when unsupported extensions to OPS are employed;
- Provides a mechanism to specify a declarative table of contents (the NCX).

6.9.2 Case Studies

Open eBook packages are used in the Publishing Industry for e-Book readers. The current members of IDPF, including organisations like the World Health Organisation, Sony, OCLC Online Computer Library Centre, are using Open eBook[128]. In Figure 28 an example of the Open Package Format is given to show the simplicity of this XML format.

```
<package version="2.0" xmlns="http://www.idpf.org/2007/opf" unique-
identifier="BookId">
  <metadata xmlns:dc="http://purl.org/dc/elements/1.1/"
xmlns:opf="http://www.idpf.org/2007/opf">
        <dc:title>Alice in Wonderland</dc:title>
        <dc:language>en</dc:language>
        <dc:identifier id="BookId"
opf:scheme="ISBN">123456789X</dc:identifier>
        <dc:creator opf:role="aut">Lewis Carroll</dc:creator>
  </metadata>

  <manifest>
        <item id="intro" href="introduction.html" media-
type="application/xhtml+xml" />
        <item id="c1" href="chapter-1.html" media-
type="application/xhtml+xml" />
```

---

[127] OPF specifications:
http://www.openebook.org/2007/opf/OPF_2.0_final_spec.html (last access on November 24th, 2008).

[128] More members can be found here:
http://www.openebook.org/membership/currentmembers.asp (last access on November 24th, 2008).

144

```
        <item id="c2" href="chapter-2.html" media-
type=application/xhtml+xml" />
        <item id="toc" href="contents.xml" media-
type="application/xhtml+xml" />
        <item id="oview" href="arch.png" media-type="image/png" />
    </manifest>

    <spine toc="ncx">
        <itemref idref="intro" />
        <itemref idref="c1" />
        <itemref idref="c1-answerkey" linear="no" />
        <itemref idref="c2" />
        <itemref idref="c2-answerkey" linear="no" />
        <itemref idref="note" linear="no" />
    </spine>

    <tours>
        <tour id="tour1" title="Chicken Recipes">
            <site title="Chicken Fingers"
href="appetizers.html#r3" />
            <site title="Chicken a la King"
href="entrees.html#r5" />
        </tour>
        <tour id="tour2" title="Vegan Recipes">
            <site title="Hummus" href ="appetizer.html#r6" />
            <site title="Lentil Casserole" href="lentils.html" />
        </tour>
    </tours>

    <guide>
        <reference type="toc" title="Table of Contents"
href="toc.html" />
        <reference type="loi" title="List Of Illustrations"
href="toc.html#figures"/>
        <reference type="other.intro" title="Introduction"
href="intro.html" />
    </guide>

</package>
```

Figure 28. Simple example of the OPF XML structure

6.9.3   Opportunities for DRIVER

The e-reader market has a high potential for growth. Offering Enhanced Publications from aggregated resources throughout Europe could be an opportunity for DRIVER to enter the e-Reader market.

6.10   Conclusion and Comparison of Package Formats

Table 13 shows an overview of the criteria which are compared to the package formats described in the following sections: MPEG21-DIDL,

METS IMS-CP, ODF packages, OOXML Open Package Convention (OPC) and the Open eBook Package Format (OPF).

In Table 13 several terms in the cells at the junctions of a criterion and a package format are used that will be explained first:

- 'Yes': the criterion is natively supported by the package format;
- 'No': the criterion is NOT natively supported by the package format AND CANNOT be extended to gain this ability;
- 'Community extensible': the criterion is NOT natively supported by the package format AND CAN be extended to gain this ability;
- 'Yes, package level': the criterion is natively supported by the package format, BUT accounts only at package level and not for the separate parts.

	MPEG21 -DIDL	METS	IMS-CP	ODF	OOXML -OPC	OPF
1. Specify parts	Yes	Yes	Yes	Yes	Yes	Yes
2. URI access of the whole (package/ manifest)	Yes	Yes	Yes	Yes	Yes	Yes
3. Ability to nest com- pound objects	Yes	Yes	Yes	Yes	Yes	No
4. Contains version information	Com- munity exten- sible	Yes	Yes	Yes	Yes	No
5. Contains descriptive attributes						
5a. Semantic type	Com- munity exten- sible	Com- munity exten- sible	Yes & commu- nity ex- tensible	Yes & com- munity exten- sible	Yes & com- munity exten- sible	No
5b. Title	Com- munity exten- sible	Com- munity exten- sible	Yes LOM	Yes	Yes	Yes

	MPEG21 -DIDL	*METS*	*IMS-CP*	*ODF*	*OOXML -OPC*	*OPF*
5c. Author	Community extensible	Community extensible	Yes LOM	Yes, package level	Yes, package level	Yes, package level
5d. Date modified	Community extensible	Yes	Yes, package level	Yes, package level	Yes, package level	Yes, package level
5e. Mime type	Yes	Yes	Yes	Yes	Yes	Yes
5f. URI	Yes	Yes	Yes	Yes	Yes	Yes
6. LTP: transformation to AIP possible	yes	Yes	Yes	No	No	No
7. Contains relationships to other parts						
7a. Containment	Yes	Yes	Yes	Yes	Yes	Yes??
7b. Sequential	Yes	Yes	Community extensible SCORM	Yes Presentation	Yes Presentation	Yes
7c. Versioning	Community extensible	Yes	Yes, LOM	Yes	Yes	No
7d. Lineage	Community extensible	Community extensible	Yes, LOM	Community extensible	Community extensible	No
7e. Manifestation	Yes	Community extensible	Yes, LOM	No	No	Yes
7f. Bibliographic Citations	Community extensible	Community extensible	Yes, LOM	Yes	Yes	No

	MPEG21-DIDL	METS	IMS-CP	ODF	OOXML-OPC	OPF
I: Package archive file specified in specifications	Yes MPEG-B, steaming	Community extensible	Yes, RFC1951 PKZIP 2.04g	Yes, ZIP	Yes, ZIP	Yes, ZIP
II: Can exist without package archive	Yes	Yes	No	No	No	No
III. Extensibility	Yes external attributes and schemas	Yes, external schemas	Yes, external schemas	No, no examples found	Yes, external schemas	No
IV. Forward and backward compatibility	Yes backward & forward	Yes, backward	No	Yes, backward	Yes, backward	No
V. Community type & size	TV and Media industry, Library and Archive Industry	Library and Archive Industry	Education Industries and E-Learning Environments (governmental and Commercial)	Governmental and Commercial Industry	Governmental, Commercial Industry, General Public (90% market share)	ePublishing Industry (a.o. OCLC) and Cultural Heritage

Table 13. Enhanced Publication recommendations and package features compared to package formats

All Package formats are useful for representing an Enhanced Publication as a Dissemination Information Package. Most of these results are gained through the ability to create different relationships among the different parts. This gives DRIVER the opportunity to harvest Enhanced Publications packaged in different formats used by different user communities. On an aggregated level, where all sources are harvested, it is possible to create relational maps between all sub-parts of the Enhanced Publications.

7. Overlays and Feeds

7.1   Introduction

These formats provide an overlay on top of an existing network of Internet resources. They tend to group references to resources, identify them and describe the content, structure and relations of all parts. The standards SWAP, ORE and POWDER are very different from each other, but were chosen for their relevance for the repository community, like ORE and SWAP, or simply, because of their innovative approach that makes them interesting for DRIVER, like POWDER.

7.2   SWAP

7.2.1   Theory of SWAP

SWAP[129] is a Dublin Core Application Profile (DCAP) to describe scholarly works. It was originally known as the eprints application profile, but its name was changed mainly to avoid confusion with the EPrints repository software[130]. The profile uses the terminology defined by the Budapest Open Access Initiative[131], so 'scholarly work' is used to refer to peer-reviewed journal articles, and also to preprints, working papers, theses, book chapters, and reports.

The overall aim of SWAP was to offer a solution to interoperability issues, which are present when using simple DC. In the UK, a key driver was to support the provision of richer and more consistent metadata for the Institute Repository Search project[132].
SWAP was developed in 2006, with funding from JISC. The development was undertaken by UKOLN and Eduserv, with input from a working group and a feedback group.

---

[129] http://www.ukoln.ac.uk/repositories/digirep/index/SWAP (last access on November 24th, 2008).

[130] http://www.eprints.org (last access on November 24th, 2008).

[131] See e.g. http://www.earlham.edu/~peters/fos/boaifaq.htm (last access on November 24th, 2008)

[132] http://www.intute.ac.uk/irs (last access on November 24th, 2008).

Scope

The scope of the work was based on JISC's specification, and included the following areas:

- Use of Dublin Core properties as far as possible, plus other necessary elements;
- Identifiers for the description and full-text(s), and for related resources;
- Support use of controlled vocabularies (subject classification, name authority, etcetera), without mandating solutions;
- Additional properties to fulfil search/browse requirements;
- Bibliographic citations and references citing other works.

Identifying Requirements

An extensive set of functional requirements[133] was developed as a result of reviews of existing work (e.g. EPrints UK project conclusions), consultation with projects and stakeholders, and input from the working group. The following were identified as principal requirements (Allinson *et al.*, 2007):

- Provision of richer, more consistent metadata;
- Facilitate search, browse or filter by a range of elements, including journal, conference or publication title, peer-review status and resource type;
- Enable identification of the latest, or most appropriate, version and facilitate navigation between different versions;
- Support added-value services, particularly those based on the use of OpenURL ContextObjects;
- Implement an unambiguous method of identifying the full-text(s);
- Enable identification of the research funder and project code;
- Identify the repository or other service making available the copy;
- Facilitate identification of open access materials;
- Support browse based on controlled vocabularies.

The Application Model - FRBR

The requirements identified above demanded a complex model. Several existing models were examined, e.g. CIDOC CRM, CERIF, with the FRBR entity-relationship model being chosen as the most suitable, for three main reasons:

---

[133] http://www.ukoln.ac.uk/repositories/digirep/index/Functional_Requirements (last access on November 24th, 2008).

150

- FRBR was developed by the library community for the entities that bibliographic records are intended to describe and the relationships between them;
- Modelling of scholarly works is working in a similar environment;
- It has the potential for wider applicability for other material types.

The FRBR model, used in the bibliographic world, contains four key entities: work, expression, manifestation and item. It also defines additional entities – 'Person', 'Corporate body', 'Concept', 'Object', 'Event' and 'Place' and the relationships between entities. Although FRBR is used as the basis for the SWAP model, some of the entity and relationship labels used in FRBR have been modified for this model, in order to make them more intuitive to those dealing with scholarly works. For example 'Scholarly work' is used instead of 'Work', 'Copy' instead of 'Item' and 'Agent' instead of 'Person' or 'Corporate body'. These changes are illustrated in Figure 29.

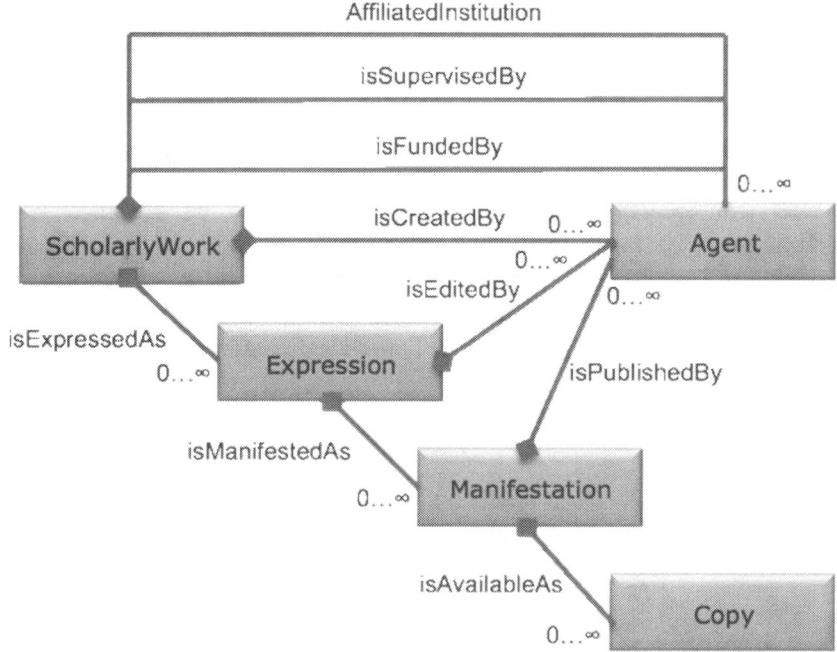

Figure 29. The SWAP model based on FRBR

A critical part of developing the application model is to identify the generic attributes that will be used to describe each entity in the model. The key attributes were therefore identified for ScholarlyWork, e.g.

title, subject, abstract, grant number, has adaptation, identifier, as well as Expression, Manifestation, Copy and Agent[134]. It is notable that using a complex underlying model such as FRBR results in relatively simple metadata and/or end-user interfaces.

DCMI Abstract Model

Whereas the model defines the entities and relationships, each entity and its relationships need to be described using an agreed set of attributes/properties. SWAP uses the DCMI Abstract Model (DCAM), which introduces the notion of 'description sets', i.e. groups of related DC descriptions. Each description contains statements about each attribute using property-value pairs. Each description set describes only one ScholarlyWork entity. However, multiple descriptions may be used to describe multiple Expression, Manifestation and Agent entities as necessary.

Application Profile and cataloguing Guidelines

The application profile provides a way of describing the attributes and relationships of each of the five entities as part of a description set. The profile also identifies mandatory elements, provides cataloguing/usage guidelines, recommendations and offers illustrative examples. The only mandatory elements are title and identifier.

The plan was to use Dublin Core properties as far as possible, with other elements as necessary. Therefore, in addition to simple DC and DC Metadata Terms, properties from other existing schemes have been used, e.g. FOAF and MARC relater codes. Five new properties have been created from scratch: grant number, affiliated institution, status, version and copyright holder.

---

[134] SWAP key attributes:
http://www.ukoln.ac.uk/repositories/digirep/index/Model (last access on November 24th, 2008).

152

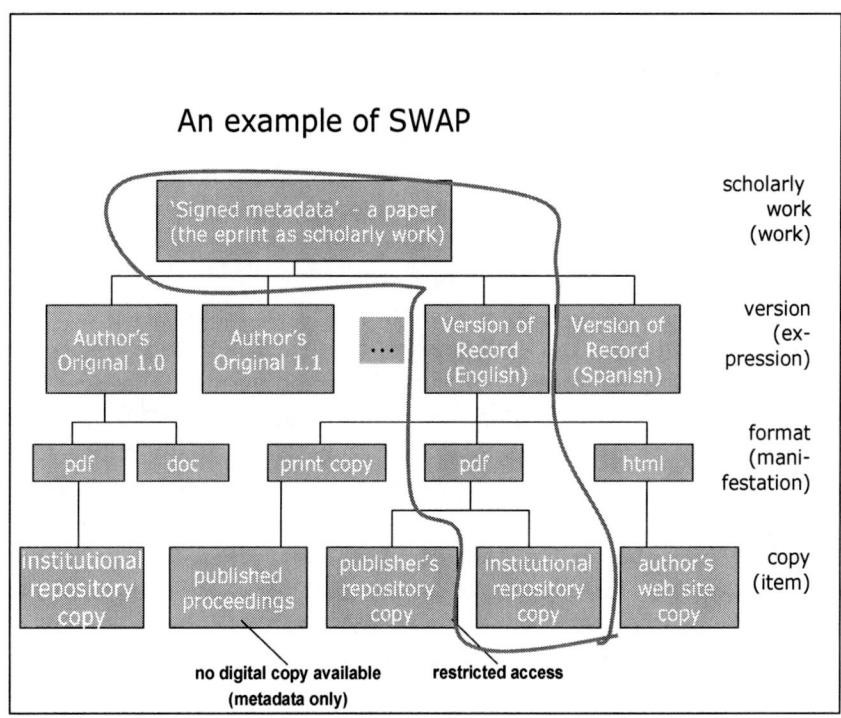

An example of SWAP

| | scholarly work (work) |

'Signed metadata' - a paper (the eprint as scholarly work)

version (ex-pression)

Author's Original 1.0 | Author's Original 1.1 | ... | Version of Record (English) | Version of Record (Spanish)

format (mani-festation)

pdf | doc | print copy | pdf | html

copy (item)

institutional repository copy | published proceedings | publisher's repository copy | institutional repository copy | author's web site copy

no digital copy available (metadata only)   restricted access

Figure 30. Example of SWAP application entities

SWAP 'sister' Profiles

Recognizing that metadata profiles were also needed for other resource types, JISC has also funded UK projects to work on three further appli-cation profiles: the Images Application Profile (IAP), the Geospatial Application Profile (GAP) and the Time-Based Media Application Profile (TBMAP). These are being developed within the relevant communities. The primary aim of developing the profiles is to improve and facilitate resource discovery.

Given that the SWAP model had met with approval in the metadata community, the new profiles were asked to base their development on SWAP as far as possible. This means they are all Dublin Core Application Profiles, i.e. based on the Dublin Core Abstract Model. They are also based on FRBR, although with some variations from the FRBR model. The profiles are at varying stages of development.

There are also two scoping studies being undertaken, looking at requirements for repositories. These are the Learning Materials

Application Profile Scoping Study, which CETIS has almost completed, and the Scientific Data Application Profile Scoping Study (UKOLN).

SWAP, IAP and TBMAP concentrate each on the description of a particular class or genre of resources. The GAP differs slightly in that it is intended to be used in conjunction with other profiles; it also focuses on a specific set of characteristics, which may be applied to resources of many different types, the distinguishing characteristic being that they have some relationship with 'place' or location.

Although an output from the bibliographic world, FRBR is intended to be capable of modelling all library holdings, including images. However the Images Application Profile project concluded that while FRBR could be used successfully to model some image types, particularly those that are the product of an artistic or intellectual process, it did not address IAP requirements (Eadie, 2008). It was also thought that FRBR's complexity could be a barrier to take-up. The IAP project had particular concerns about the FRBR notion of an abstract Expression layer in the model and it was decided to omit this entity from the current version of the IAP model. As a result of omitting this layer, it could be argued that the IAP does not conform to FRBR. It is however possible that Expression could be re-instated in a future version. This is still under discussion.

A 'core' Application Profile?
If repositories expose metadata records based on DCAPs such as SWAP and IAP, then other services, e.g. DRIVER, can aggregate those records and offer functionality across the merged dataset. Harmonisation of the profiles is important for interoperability and implementation purposes and the projects are working closely together. Repositories are likely to have mixed content, so they would potentially need to use several profiles.

Support from the repository software providers is needed to facilitate implementation – if the profiles are already implemented within the software then repository managers will be able to expose SWAP or IAP enabled records easily. However it is unrealistic to expect that software providers implement multiple varying profiles: it also increases the level of complexity managed by aggregators.

As a result of recent discussions it has been suggested that the APs should converge on a single XML schema with points of extensibility for different types of material. This is still under discussion at the time of writing and will be taken forward by JISC and UKOLN. The importance of developing exemplars is also recognised, so that repositories, software developers and other stakeholders can see what services could look like.

Implementation and Support

JISC is providing resources to support the take-up of the application profiles in the UK. Alongside this JISC is also funding development work by the DSpace Foundation in the UK, which will include developing SWAP capability 'out-of-the-box'. The EPrints software has a facility for exporting SWAP records only.

Despite the fact that SWAP is seen as a successful development and is very well received in the community, there has been very little proper implementation as yet. While there are no services demonstrating the benefits, repositories are reluctant to make the effort to provide the metadata, but without the metadata no services can be developed. This 'chicken and egg' situation could potentially be addressed by developing demonstrators to test specific requirements identified by repository managers.

DCMI Scholarly Communications Community

The DCMI Scholarly Communications Community[135] is a forum for individuals and organisations to exchange information, knowledge and general discussion on issues relating to using Dublin Core for describing research papers, scholarly texts, data objects and other resources created and used within scholarly communications. This includes providing a forum for discussion around SWAP and for other existing and future application profiles created to describe items of scholarly communication. A workshop was held at DC-2008 in Berlin, which included discussion on taking SWAP forward.

The DCMI Usage Board has also carried out a review of SWAP – SWAP was used to test the new DCAP review criteria. As a result there are a few minor alterations to be made to SWAP. Following this, SWAP will move to the DCMI website.

---

[135] http://dublincore.org/groups/scholar (last access on November 24th, 2008).

7.2.2 Case studies of SWAP

Case Study of CLADDIER

As indicated, SWAP has not yet been fully implemented; the CLADDIER case study therefore describes a 'partial' implementation. The CLADDIER project[136], which ended in 2007, investigated the issue of linking publications held in institutional repositories to the underlying data held in specialist repositories, by developing the theme of citations, not only for publications but also for datasets. It built a demonstration system linking publications held in two institutional repositories (Southampton University and the CCLRC) with data holdings in the British Atmospheric Data Centre. The CLADDIER 'track-back' mechanism allows repositories to inform each other about deposits. It uses SWAP to exchange information about the citation/scholarly work. SWAP was chosen in order to provide a richer information model, with citations broken down into fields, which could then be used to offer greater flexibility and functionality.

> *"Within [the SWAP] application profile, there are a number of fields for representing bibliographicCitation and references. While these fields were not exactly corresponding to the meaning we define them in the CLADDIER project, the correspondence is sufficiently close to use to represent forward and backward citations in our model.*
>
> *The whole of the [SWAP] application profile proved too large and as a model for citations alone, it had too much unnecessary detail. As a consequence, for demonstration purposes, a small number of fields were selected. [...]*
>
> *Thus with these fields, most of the key information for citation of at least journal articles is represented. Data citations can also be adapted to comply with this format. This model was then implemented within the ePubs data model itself. This required the modification of the ePubs database schema in a number of different places, and the implementation of a number of database triggers to maintain the consistency of the model."* (Matthews *et al.*, 2007).

---

[136] http://claddier.badc.ac.uk/trac (last access on November 24th, 2008).

Case Study of WRAP, University of Warwick

Again, as SWAP has not yet been fully implemented, the WRAP case study describes a 'partial' implementation. The Warwick Research Archive Project (WRAP[137]) aims to establish, populate and promote an institutional repository service for the university's written research output, including pre- and post-prints as well as e-theses. It has been funded by JISC for 18 months, until March 2009.

The project chose to use SWAP because they believed it was most suited to the scholarly content they aim to include, and would result in rich, high quality metadata, which in turn would mean better interoperability and improved retrieval. The university was keen to demonstrate a quality implementation. It is also hoped that being at the cutting edge on metadata schema and creating rich consistent records, will allow the repository to take advantage of new technologies as and when they become available. In the future it might be possible to use the rich metadata created to link between citations, or to present WRAP records alongside records from other data sources such as the library catalogue to provide a more complete record of academics' publications[138].

It was therefore necessary to configure the EPrints software used at Warwick, specifically on the input and display sides, to take SWAP. This meant a large amount of customisation. The lack of documentation about EPrints and what each file does was a hindrance. The configuration was a resource-intensive process. The types were changed to fit the SWAP document type vocabulary, which then had a knock-on effect for workflows, etcetera. A large number of SWAP fields lacking in generic EPrints were also added.

However they believe that:

> "The real problem is that of integrating a hierarchical model like SWAP into a flat structure like EPrints. Also, I don't believe that the creation of a SWAP plug-in, as we have, really amounts to a SWAP implementation. If the rich SWAP metadata is lacking then the SWAP plug-in can't really do that much." [139]

---

[137] http://wrap.warwick.ac.uk/ (last access on December 11th, 2008).

[138] Jenny Delasalle, University of Warwick, email communication on September 19th, 2008.

[139] Stuart Hunt, University of Warwick, email communication on May 13th, 2008.

There is also some concern that it takes at least two hours to process a single item into the repository, while records are currently created by cataloguers. However this is not necessarily a SWAP-related issue.

7.2.3 Opportunities for DRIVER

Having been developed in 2006, it could be argued that SWAP was ahead of its time. There have been suggestions that it is too complex, given its basis in FRBR. One possible solution is to develop a 'SWAP Lite' version, with a two layer model instead of the four layers as in FRBR. There is likely to be support in the community for a 'Lite' version.

Implementation of the SWAP hierarchical model by repository software developers needs to happen as a first step, so repositories can implement an 'out of the box' SWAP solution. It is unrealistic and unsustainable for repository managers to carry out extensive customisation locally. Therefore SWAP records are unlikely to be routinely available for harvesting by repository aggregators for some time to come. Opportunities for DRIVER to benefit from SWAP are therefore limited in the foreseeable future. However, DRIVER should maintain a watching brief to monitor future uptake.

7.3 ORE, Object Reuse and Exchange

7.3.1 Theory of OAI-ORE

The Object Reuse and Exchange (OAI-ORE) standard is a new data exchange model proposed by the Open Archives Group. At the time of writing this report, the standard was still in beta version, i.e. 0.9 (Lagoze *et al.*, 2008a), but version 1.0 (Lagoze *et al.*, 2008b) became available before the report was completed. This standard was developed to allow for the aggregation of web resources. OAI-ORE provides the means to express the complex nature of publications composed out of metadata records, full text and auxiliary files (Lagoze *et al.*, 2008c).

The collection of resources that make up a scholarly publication is called an Aggregation, each resource in an Aggregation is an Aggregated Resource. Using URI's, Aggregations can unambiguously be identified and used as new type of resource in Semantic Web applications. In order to instantiate, describe and identify Aggregations, OAI-ORE defines Resource Maps, which also provide information about the context in which an Aggregation was defined. It is possible to define the

Aggregation creator, the date it was published and under which license conditions.

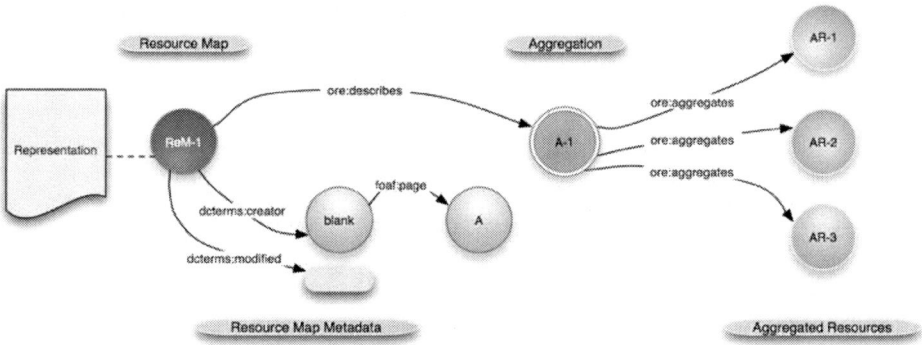

Figure 31. The OAI-ORE basic model

This model is showing an Aggregation containing three Aggregated Resources described by a Resource Map (source:http://www.openarchives.org/ore/1.0/primer).

OAI-ORE suggests many published models for ORE documents using Atom, RDF/XML, OAI-PMH, and RDFa. In the following technical sections the RDF/XML format will be explained.

Aggregation
In OAI-ORE, Internet resources are grouped by an 'Aggregation'. The components of an Aggregation are called the 'Aggregated Resources' and are listed by simple enumeration. Using the RDF/XML serialisation of OAI-ORE, an Aggregation can be represented by an RDF Description of the type 'Aggregation'. Aggregated resources are added using ORE 'aggregates' properties (Lagoze and Van de Sompel, 2007).

```
<rdf:Description rdf:about="http://arxiv.org/aggregation/astro-
ph/0601007">

 <rdf:type
rdf:resource="http://www.openarchives.org/ore/terms/Aggregation"/>

 <ore:aggregates rdf:resource=
"http://arxiv.org/ps/astro-ph/0601007"/>

 <ore:aggregates rdf:resource=
"http://arxiv.org/pdf/astro-ph/0601007"/>

 <ore:aggregates rdf:resource=
"http://arxiv.org/ps/astro-ph/0601008"/>

</rdf:Description>
```

Figure 32. A simple OAI-ORE aggregation containing three resources

Figure 32 shows an example of such an Aggregation. Three resources are aggregated, the first two resources represent the PS and PDF version of an article in the arXiv with identifier '061007'. The third resource is a related article with identifier '0601008'. Metadata about an Aggregation can be included by adding RDF triples. For instance, to express that this aggregation can be referenced with a DOI identifier, the 'similarTo' term from the ORE vocabulary can be used.

```
<rdf:Description rdf:about="http://arxiv.org/aggregation/astro-
ph/0601007">

 <rdf:type
rdf:resource="http://www.openarchives.org/ore/terms/Aggregation"/>

 <ore:similarTo rdf:resource=
  "info:doi/10.1045/february-2006-smith"/>

 <ore:aggregates rdf:resource=
  "http://arxiv.org/ps/astro-ph/0601007"/>

 <ore:aggregates rdf:resource=
  "http://arxiv.org/pdf/astro-ph/0601007"/>

 <ore:aggregates rdf:resource="http://arxiv.org/ps/astro-
ph/0601008"/>

</rdf:Description>
```

Figure 33. An annotated OAI-ORE Aggregation

Figure 33 shows how the vocabulary term 'ore:similarTo' is added to the Aggregation. RDF allows the inclusion of terms from any vocabulary to add metadata to resources. Dublin Core terms could be added to provide descriptive metadata. PREMIS terms could be added to give archival metadata needed for long-term preservation. OAI-ORE provides no restrictions on the vocabulary terms to be used. Using the same technique, metadata can be added to Aggregated Resources. To do this, new Descriptors need to be added to the RDF/XML document:

```
<rdf:Description rdf:about=
 "http://arxiv.org/aggregation/astro-ph/0601007">
  [...]
</rdf:Description>

<rdf:Description rdf:about=
   "http://arxiv.org/ps/astro-ph/0601007">
  <dcterms:hasFormat rdf:resource=
   "http://arxiv.org/pdf/astro-ph/0601007"/>
</rdf:Description>

<rdf:Description rdf:about="http://arxiv.org/pdf/astro-ph/0601007">
  <dcterms:hasFormat rdf:resource=
   "http://arxiv.org/ps/astro-ph/0601007"/>
</rdf:Description>
```

Figure 34. Annotated OAI-ORE Aggregation Resources

Figure 34 shows how metadata are added to the first two Aggregated Resources by creating two new Descriptors and adding Dublin Core vocabulary terms to it. This RDF/XML fragment expresses the relationship between two resources. The first PS resource is said to be a different format of the second PDF resource and vice versa. Like in the case of Aggregations, any vocabulary term can be added to add more metadata about each separate resource.

Resource Map

To describe the Aggregation-as-a-whole, an OAI-ORE Resource Map needs to be constructed. The Resource Map (ReM) is an RDF file, which contains metadata about itself. Using a self-referencing technique, metadata are added to the complete graph represented by the Resource Map file.

```
<RDF>

 <rdf:Description rdf:about="">
  <dc:creator rdf:resource=
   "http://example.org/agents/AgencyX"/>
  <dc:rights rdf:resource=
   "http://creativecommons.org/licenses/by/2.0/be/"/>
  [...]
 </rdf:Description>

 <rdf:Description rdf:about="... /aggregation/...">
  [...]
 </rdf:Description>

 <rdf:Description rdf:about="... /ps/.../0601007">
  [...]
 </rdf:Description>

 <rdf:Description about="..../pdf/.../0601007">
  [...]
 </rdf:Description>

</RDF>
```

Figure 35: An OAI-ORE Resource Map

Figure 35 shows how the Descriptors describing the Aggregation and Aggregated Resources are added to a Resource Map file. The Resource Map is described by its own descriptor. Here, the metadata expresses that 'AgencyX' is the creator of the aggregation and attaches a Creative Commons license to it.

Formal Semantics

Formally, the OAI-ORE metadata model is based on RDF. The RDF model defines the syntax and semantics to describe web resources. RDF can express relations between resources and provides the means to add properties to each separate resource. It has a very expressive power with layered semantics on top of which ontology, rules, logic and formal proof of statements can be defined. Not only web resources can be described but also abstract concepts.

Each resource is identified by an URI, which can be used as the name of a web resource or abstract concept, but also as a resource location. By de-referencing resource URI's new RDF representations for the resources can be obtained, creating a web of interlinked RDF resources called the Semantic Web, similar to the World Wide Web of interlinked HTML documents.

162

RDF properties can be added using the RDF Schema language, which defines vocabularies of terms to be used in RDF statements. The OAI-ORE vocabulary of relationships defines 8 terms: aggregates, isAggregatedBy, describes, isDescribedBy, lineage, proxyFor, proxyIn and similarTo. Together with terms from the OWL (McGuinness and van Harmelen, 2004) and Dublin Core vocabularies, rich descriptions can be created for resources.

In OAI-ORE two URI's are important:
1. URI-R, the URI used to reference the Resource Map, e.g. http://inst.org/rem.rdf;
2. URI-A, the URI used to reference an Aggregation. In the examples above the URI-A of the Aggregation would be the RDF/XML document location of the Resource Map appended with the value of the 'rdf:about' attribute of the Aggregation, e.g. http://inst.org/rem.rdf#aggregation.

Using OAI-ORE semantics, the URI-A should be used when referencing an Aggregation, for instance a publication, a list of images, a website. The URI-R should be used to reference a descriptive representation of the Aggregation, which indicates, for instance, who created the Aggregation, at what date, and under which license (Van de Sompel, 2008).

7.3.2 Case Studies

Being a recent development, the size of the OAI-ORE user community is very hard to tell, since it is not yet an established one[140]. But it is very obvious that it is gaining momentum in the digital library/repository world. For this report, inspiration was drawn from the experiments presented during the OAI-ORE Open Meetings at John Hopkins University[141] and University of Southampton[142] on March 3 and April 4,

---

[140] Rob Sanderson remarks: It's hard to tell; however there are a number of people blogging about it who are quite far removed from initially targeted audiences of repositories.
The libraries that Foresite has produced have so far been downloaded more than 70 times. (http://code.google.com/p/foresite-toolkit/downloads/list, last access on November 24th, 2008) which is encouraging that not only are people looking at the specification, they're also motivated to do things with it.
[141] http://www.openarchives.org/ore/meetings/hopkins/agenda.htm (last access on November 24th, 2008).

2008 respectively. Information specialists use the new model in a number of applications.

1. *OAI-ORE experiments* at the University of Illinois Library at Urbana-Champaign. Timothy Cole and his colleagues are looking into ways to associate multiple web resources that are to be considered as part of a larger whole (Cole, 2008):

    i)   use of OAI-ORE to tie together different views or representations of what is intellectually a single image resource, e.g. the thumbnail view, the high-resolution view, and the in-context view of a single digitised photograph, by creating a ReM and serializing as an ATOM feed. This is very relevant as a potential next step in their work on the Digital Library Federation (DLF) Aquifer Asset Action activity (Chavez et al., 2006).

    ii) use of OAI-ORE to reveal the structure of a digitised book and associated objects such as annotations of parts of such books. Hence they created ReMs that enumerate separately addressable parts of a book and are also looking at ReMs that can tie an individual annotation to multiple granular, i.e. page-level or lower, targets across different representations of the same book or even across multiple books or editions.

2. *OAI-ORE for publishing workflows.* At the Digital Research and Curation Center of the Sheridan Libraries (John Hopkins University), Tim DiLauro and colleagues are using OAI-ORE in relation to data archiving for journals of the American Astronomical Society (AAS). Future developments include the integration of their work into the workflow of AAS, the integration of ReM packaging into office platforms and the search for new functionalities (DiLauro, 2008).

3. *Client-side preservation techniques for ORE aggregations.* Michael Nelson and colleagues (Old Dominion University) base their work on the preservation of information inside the web infrastructure on the premise that ReMs are critical for that purpose. Websites may be reconstructed or recovered with web resources found in several archives and caches. In view of preservation, the ReM of the recovered web resources defines members of the aggregations and

---

[142] http://www.openarchives.org/ore/meetings/Soton/agenda.htm (last access on November 24th, 2008).

relationships between them. A number of techniques for harvesting, migration, validation and auditing are run on the server-side, yet interaction with the end-users in the process should improve the quality of the results. A wiki serving as an inter-client message store could function as a human and computer readable revision control system for ReMs (Nelson and Koneru, 2008).

4. *Portfolios, a framework for time-critical automated decisions.* Countless astronomical phenomena are registered by numerous sky survey systems. All the resulting information has to be filtered, published and managed in a network of participants, resulting in a heterogeneous collection of source material and derived information in different media formats and different network locations that has to be human and machine operable. The data relationships are significant for classification. Matthew J. Graham (Caltech) and colleagues use OAI-ORE to describe aggregations of data objects as named graphs143 and serialise them as ReMs. Hence OAI-ORE provides them with a framework for their portfolios (Graham, 2008).

5. *The SCOPE system, Scientific Compound Object Publishing and Editing.* Jane Hunter and colleagues (The University of Queensland) apply OAI-ORE in the scientific publication process, including the availability of raw and derivative data, sharing of several services, enabling review, and validation, to allow scientists to *"easily author, publish and edit scientific compound objects"*. Their objectives include a tool for authoring compound objects, interactive GUI to link component from different locations, label relationships, coming to publish and RSS notification. Export or output in different formats is supported and the compound objects are published as files within a Fedora digital library (Cheung et al., 2007; Cheung and Hunter, 2008).

6. *Preview of the TheOREM project.* Jim Downing and colleagues (University of Cambridge) are aiming to demonstrate strengths and expose weaknesses of OAI-ORE that is the research subject of

---

[143] It should be noted, however, although Named Graphs (http://www.w3.org/2004/03/trix, last access on November 24th, 2008) was one of the concepts at the origin of ORE, that this precise approach was omitted from the release version 1.0 of the ORE specifications (as announced by Herbert Van de Sompel, personal communication, on August 22nd, 2008).

TheOREM, a project for description and submission of complex thesis objects as part of a semantic web approach. If proven useful, they will probably include it in developments of their linked open data projects such as Crystaleye144). The development work, for which 6 months of a postdoc are foreseen, could benefit of the Foresite145 project tools if proven useful. Sesame and Jena will likely be used for RDF indexing and handling, but undoubtedly, a fair amount of code development will also be involved (Downing, 2008)[146].

7. *Functional ORE: supporting information topology experiments and archival description.* Rob Sanderson, University of Liverpool, UK, uses OAI-ORE for two purposes. One is Foresite, a JISC-funded project in the field of repositories and scholarly communication. The other is as a cross-domain, interoperable method for describing archives. Currently most archival finding aids are generated using a DTD called EAD, however this is very specific to the archival domain. ORE provides a more general and no less descriptive method to allow the reuse and exchange of the collection and item descriptions. Plans include building a crosswalk set of style sheets between EAD and ORE to enable current generation systems to export their descriptions using ORE (Sanderson *et al.*, 2008).

8. *ORE serialisation of objects based on Fedora model.* Ben O'Steen at Oxford University describes repository objects in terms of the original Fedora model and the terms of the ORE serialisations. By maintaining this modelling as the object moves between systems, the actual software that holds them becomes less important. One of the projects he is implementing is to synchronise the contents of an EPrints repository into a Fedora system, which is part of the overall archive, 'federated' to an extent. He considers OAI-ORE to be an enabling technology and, as such, part of the Semantic Web movement, hence he conceives the OAI-ORE community as being part of the larger Semantic Web (Linked Data, SWIG) community.

9. *Java libraries at the Swedish National Library.* Oskar Grenholm at the Swedish National library is working together with LANL and

---

[144] http://wwmm.ch.cam.ac.uk/crystaleye (last access on November 24th, 2008).
[145] http://foresite.cheshire3.org (last access on November 24th, 2008).
[146] Additional comments obtained through personal communication by email with Jim Downing in June 2008.

Fedora Commons to implement reference implementations of a Java library for OAI-ORE. The long-term plan is to be able to receive deposited e-material to the Swedish National library in OAI-ORE format.

10. *DRIVER II OAI-ORE Demonstrator.* Maarten Hoogerwerf (DANS) and Arjan Hogenaar (KNAW) have developed in close collaboration with the other members of the DRIVER-community a Demonstrator of Enhanced Publications under the terms of the DRIVER II programme. Existing Enhanced Publications have already been rewritten in OAI-ORE. In order to realise interoperability, the OAI-ORE documents have been serialised in RDF. RDF was chosen because of its flexibility and its extensibility. Besides, RDF facilitates a sophisticated way to describe the relations between the components of an Enhanced Publication. The Demonstrator will be used as a source of inspiration for the development of a new service for Enhanced Publications in DRIVER II.

From the above examples[147] it is clear that information specialists are using OAI-ORE exactly what it is meant for, to connect various web resources into an 'intellectually' single resource. Their motivation lies in the enhancement of digital scholarly communications and inter-operability between digital scholarly communication systems, or the integration of data capture with existent workflow for multiple journals and the need to capture relationships with resources which are not part of a particular article.

Further arguments mentioned in favour of OAI-ORE include:
- The improvement of the ingestion and reuse of the contents in a research archive, compared to free-text on HTML pages or OAI-PMH with DC;
- Its more sharp and exclusive focus on a specific problem space, in comparison to existing Semantic Web standards and more library-specific standards;
- The possibility to isolate and work on the issues most relevant for defining boundaries and reusable components of complex, compound information resources;

---

[147] The observations and comments in this and the following paragraphs are based on personal communication (mostly by e-mail, but also face-to-face) with Tim Cole, Jim Downing, Oskar Grenholm, Ben O'Steen, Rob Sanderson and Herbert Van de Sompel in the period May to August 2008.

- Disaggregation of content packages allowing better use of standard web technologies and techniques with content, and the pass-by-reference nature of OAI-ORE;
- The fact that it leverages significant Semantic Web work and the work of communities like those using ATOM.

Yet, there may be some aspects to watch out for. Collaborators of the above case studies raised several elements:
- The challenge to capture relationships among conceptual objects and web resources and the need to adjust, in retrospective, some tools that people have been using;
- Among the hardest tasks is to model resources consisting of multiple URI-addressable sub-resources correctly, and to know what additional semantics are needed and when to use existing semantics;
- The need exists to develop community consensus on a number of issues and on tools that will exploit and help verify and validate ReM instances;
- Problem-space may prove to be too narrowly defined and/or not critical enough to scholarly communication at this point in time;
- Other primary concerns involve the provenance and fixity issues created when pass-by-reference is used.

The greatest risk, as with any new protocol designed to facilitate interoperability, is that the protocol gets no acceptance in the wider community. Where is interoperability if only one organisation is using the protocol? The strong support for the OAI-PMH protocol by libraries however, could easily lead to adoption of OAI-ORE standards and the planned future support of Fedora for OAI-ORE will create a further stimulus.

Even at a time when the first full version of OAI-ORE was being expected, tools were already made available. For the Foresite project two software libraries were written, with a lot of code on top of them, and downloaded relatively many times[148] in a short time span. This is an encouraging idea for the further development of the ORE-community. These libraries are being used also in another of the above study cases and integrated in the systems implemented over there.

---

[148] At the time of the first draft of this report (May 2008), seventy times.

The choice for OAI-ORE is often made because of it is in line with the web architecture, unlike a monolithic XML structure. One respondent saw no direct competitors for ORE serialisations because of the unique characteristics of self-descriptiveness. Another states ORE is best fitted for his purpose, and has no direct competitors, since it is the only one in tune with the web architecture and the massively distributed web graph.

Some aspects of ORE however, overlap existing technologies. Possibly there is some competition with SWORD. ATOM and other Semantic Web approaches arguably could be adapted in idiosyncratic ways to do much of what OAI-ORE allows to do, but then it would only enhance interoperability to the extent that others adopt the same specific approach. In the library world, there is some overlap of ORE with METS, but METS is not well known outside the library community and comes with additional overhead to address other, more library-specific needs. The CIDOC-CRM standard is said to be too complicated. It has been around for 10 years and has not progressed much.

Yet, while OAI-ORE serialises in ATOM and RDF, it is important to recognise that ORE adds new semantics, useful in exploiting and managing multi-part resources. While well rooted in existing technologies, ORE offers an opportunity to advance the current state-of-the-art.

7.3.3   Opportunities for DRIVER

OAI-ORE is an asset for DRIVER. Preliminary assessment of results so far suggests that ReMs may be useful for many applications, for instance as a way to maintain across distributed repositories well-ordered, identified, and typed relationships between components of digitised books that are being processed in a de-centralised way. This processing can be done by both by humans, e.g. in distributed proof-reading or lemma marking correction, and by machines, e.g. in statistical analyses of lemmas found in the book's text, stored in a different location than where the digital book is stored. Because the uptake of OAI-ORE in the repository and digital library community is quite large, and the DRIVER demonstrator for EP's uses ORE as a technology, OAI-ORE will probably become one of the leading technologies for dealing with EP's within DRIVER.

7.4   POWDER

7.4.1   Theory

POWDER, or the Protocol for Web Description Resources, is a new W3C working draft providing means for individuals or organisations to describe a group of resources through the publication of machine-readable metadata documents (Smith *et al.*, 2008). Authors of POWDER documents publish files containing descriptions of multiple resources available on the World Wide Web. Groups of resources can be described as a whole by enumerating the individual items, or matching URI's against descriptions of the URI's schemes used. This is in contrast with OAI-ORE, where resources can be grouped only by listing individual items. The aim of POWDER is to provide a platform through which opinions, claims and assertions about online resources can be expressed by people and exchanged by machines[149]. POWDER takes a very broad approach so that it is possible for both the resource creator and third parties to make assertions about all kinds of things, with no architectural limits on the kind of thing they are making claims about[150].

Resource Sets

Internet resources are grouped by means of 'iriset' sections. In these sections, resources can be grouped not only by listing all its elements but also by describing the characteristics of the resource URI. Using this technique, assertions can be made on aggregations of dynamic and static resources. For instance:

```
<iriset>
  <includeresources>
      http://some.inst.org/pub1.html
      http://some.inst.org/pub1.pdf
      http://some.inst.org/pub1/image1.gif
      http://some.inst.org/pub1/image2.jpg
  </includeresources>
</iriset>
```

is an example of an iriset which groups resources by listing all its elements. In this case, the hypothetical publication 'pub1' on the

---

[149] http://realworldxml.blogspot.com/2008/03/protocol-for-web-description-resources.html (last access on November 24th, 2008).

[150] http://xml.coverpages.org/newsletter/news2007-09-26.html (last access on November 24th, 2008).

'some.institute.org' website. Using wildcards, an assertion can be made on all publications on the 'some.institute.org' website:

```
<iriset>
   <includeregex>
        http://some.inst.org/pub.*
   </includeregex>
</iriset>
```

In this example, all URI's starting with 'http://some.institute.org/pub' are included in the group.

POWDER constrains the elements in the group by describing the characteristics of resources URI's with the syntax:

```
scheme://host:port/path/?query
```

as shown below:

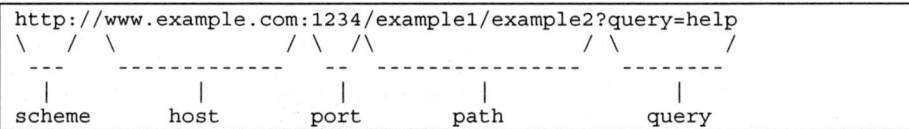

Figure 36. Example of POWDER syntax

POWDER uses the '<includeschemes>' element to group resources by URI scheme. To group by host, POWDER uses the '<includehosts>' element. The POWDER draft provides an exhaustive list of grouping elements. To group by wildcards, POWDER uses regular expressions, as shown in the example above.

Describing Resource Sets
Every 'iriset' must have one 'descriptorset', which describes the resources in the 'iriset'. These 'descriptorsets' contain arbitrary RDF/XML that describe the 'irisets' but can also carry textual and/or graphical summaries that can be displayed to end users.

The following example creates an iriset containing the aggregation of resources that make up a publication with title 'On the Electrodynamics of Moving Bodies' by Albert Einstein. When a summary of the iriset needs to be displayed, the text 'Einstein's article on special relativity' is used.

```
<dr>
  <iriset>
   <includeresources>
       http://some.inst.org/pub1.html
       http://some.inst.org/pub1.pdf
       http://some.inst.org/pub1/image1.gif
       http://some.inst.org/pub1/image2.jpg
   </includeresources>
  </iriset>
  <descriptorset>
     <dc:title>On the Electrodynamics of Moving
Bodies</dc:title>
     <dc:creator>Einstein, Albert</dc:creator>
     <dc:date>1905</dc:date>
     <dc:identifier>info:doi/10.21821/journal.x.sda0.121
     <displaytext>
       Einstein's article on special relativity
     </displaytext>
</descriptorset>
</dr>
```

Figure 37. Iriset containing the aggregation of resources that make up the publication 'On the Electrodynamics of Moving Bodies' by Albert Einstein

Complete Example

```
<?xml version="1.0"?>
<powder  xmlns="http://www.w3.org/2007/05/powder# ">
  <attribution>
   <maker>http://authority.example.org/foaf.rdf#me</maker>
   <issued>2007-12-14</issued>
   <validfrom>2008-01-01</validfrom>
   <validuntil>2008-12-31</validuntil>
  </attribution>
     <dr>
   <iriset>
   <includeresources>
       http://some.inst.org/pub1.html
       http://some.inst.org/pub1.pdf
       http://some.inst.org/pub1/image1.gif
       http://some.inst.org/pub1/image2.jpg
   </includeresources>
  </iriset>
  <descriptorset>
     <dc:title>On the Electrodynamics of Moving Bodies</dc:title>
     <dc:creator>Einstein, Albert</dc:creator>
     <dc:date>1905</dc:date>
     <dc:identifier>info:doi/10.21821/journal.x.sda0.121
     <displaytext>
      Einstein's article on special relativity
     </displaytext>
  </descriptorset>
  </dr>
</powder>
```

Figure 38. A complete POWDER document

By adding an 'attribution' section, a complete POWDER document can be created. The attribution element contains the information about who has provided the description, and typically, will also include information about when it was created and any validity period.

Formal Semantics

The POWDER operational semantics shown above are underpinned by more formal semantics. With GRDDL transformations, POWDER documents can be transformed into a Semantic POWDER document. These POWDER-S documents are valid RDF/OWL documents that can be processed by Semantic Web tools that implement the extensions of the POWDER resource grouping.

7.4.2 Case Studies

Phil Archer (FOSI, Family Online Safety Institute)[151] uses the POWDER standards for trust signs and verification[152]. The goal is to identify digital resources for different audiences by using trust marks. These can be commercial users, like Vodafone/ Deutsche Telekom/ Operasoftware, or social groups like children's safety. The ultimate goal is to bring the appropriate content to the right audience. This is similar to DRIVER's goal. POWDER is a W3C working group[153] and was born out of some preliminary trust mark projects for medical sites[154]. There isn't an official user community yet, as POWDER is still in development at the time of writing (June 2008), but many scientific and commercial partners, mostly in the AI and computer science field, are interested. The first software release in September 2008 may bring about many new implementations and new tool developments. POWDER was preferred over OAI-ORE because it allows writing about many resources at once. Rob Sanderson[155] explains that ORE, being based on RDF, does not allow asserting the same predicate and object across many subjects in a single statement, i.e. to set the same metadata property on multiple things at once.

---

[151] http://www.fosi.org/cms (last access on November 24th, 2008).

[152] http://www.w3.org/2005/Incubator/wcl (last access on November 24th, 2008).

[153] http://www.w3.org/2007/powder (last access on November 24th, 2008).

[154] http://www.w3.org/PICS, http://www.icra.org/systemspecification (for both last access on November 24th, 2008).

[155] Personal communication, August 11th, 2008.

	ORE	POWDER
Aim	To define aggregations of resources	To provide descriptions of groups of resources
Attribution	Mandatory Dc: creator is used.	Mandatory Foaf:maker is used.
Temporal data	Present	Present
Resource Grouping	By enumeration	By IRI component matching
Tension with Semantic Web	-	Defines a semantic extension plus a GRDDL transform to go from operational semantics in XML to Formal semantics in RDF/OWL. Requires processing to get a description of a given resource.

Figure 39. A comparison of ORE versus POWDER based on theory and case studies

7.4.3   Opportunities for DRIVER

POWDER can be an alternative way to present aggregations to the Semantic Web. DRIVER could use POWDER techniques for trust marks and quality labelling of scientific datasets. This way, quality data sets can be oriented towards the targeted public, an important feature for DRIVER.

POWDER is also being looked into for the DRIVER II Demonstrator of Enhanced Publications, as a way to add metadata to an Enhanced Publication consisting out of dynamic datasets. In a way, POWDER behaves in the opposite way of OAI-ORE. Whereas in OAI-ORE you look at an aggregation and want to learn about the specific resources in it, in POWDER you look at the resource and want to learn to which aggregations it belongs, and which properties they add to the resource. POWDER is a viable alternative for ORE when the aggregations have a very dynamic nature or can't be simply enumerated.

8.   Embedding

8.1   Introduction

Whereas the packages and overlays categories introduced new formats, the characteristic of 'embedding' technologies is the 'internality' of the added semantic annotations. For example, by adding semantic highlights in the html of a splash page, the PDF link to the document is better discernable for machines through the embedded annotation. Microformats revitalise some older html tag, which get a new, richer, semantic meaning. This way, no extra data or format needs to be added, and the content becomes richer through the embedded information. Whilst other similar technologies, such as RDFa (Adida *et al.*, 2008), and XMP (Adobe, 2005) exist, microformats are gaining many adopters like Yahoo, Word Press, and Flickr, because of their simplicity.

8.2   Microformats

8.2.1   Microformats Theory

Designed for humans first and machines second, microformats are a set of simple data formats that build on existing and widely used Internet standards[156]. The proposed standards augment existing (X)HTML pages with semantically rich content that can be used in automatic processing by software agents. The core of microformats is to solve real existing problems starting with simple, existing standards. Being embeddable and modular, microformats allow for decentralised development (Allsopp, 2007). In the search for solutions for existing problems, microformats have taken a bottom-up approach. Instead of starting a standardisation track proposing new metadata standards, simple seemingly ad-hoc solutions are being proposed which are popularised by massive adaptation. Started at grassroots level, microformats have gained interest by companies such as Google, Microsoft and Yahoo. Browser implementations are available as plug-ins or by default in the next versions of Firefox[157] and Internet Explorer[158].

---

[156] http://microformats.org/about (last access on November 24th, 2008).

[157] http://ejohn.org/blog/microformats-in-firefox-3 (last access on November 24th, 2008).

Microformats add semantic information to (X)HTML pages, which can be processed by software agents. Added microformat annotations can contain simple or structured values.

In its simplest form, microformats add semantics to HTML links. To do this, microformats take the advantage of existing 'rel' attributes in HMTL. By adding a controlled vocabulary to the values of these attributes, semantically rich web pages are created.

As an example, a license statement can be added to a web page by using the 'rel-license' microformat. This format includes in HTML anchors a 'rel' attribute with value 'license' as in:

```
<a href="http://creativecommons.org/licenses/2.5" rel="license">
   Creative Commons Attribution version 2.5
</a>
```

Figure 40. A machine-readable CC license

Using this microformat, a human and machine-readable license is linked to the webpage. The HTML anchor provides for a human visitor a displayable text for the license.

Creative Commons Attribution version 2.5

Figure 41. A human readable CC license

The rel='license' indicates for a machine that a license with URI 'http://creativecommons.org/licenses/2.5' is applicable to the webpage. Services such as Google and Yahoo scan HTML pages for these 'rel' attributes and use them in applications such as 'Google Creative Commons Search' and 'Yahoo Creative Commons Search' (see Figure 42).

---

[158]http://factoryjoe.com/blog/2006/10/29/internet-explorer-80-will-support-microformats (last access on November 24th, 2008).

Figure 42. Yahoo Creative Commons Search uses rel-license microformats

Other popular link-based microformats:

- Rel-tag, used to add Flickr and del.icios.us style tagging information to webpages;
- VoteLinks, used for endorsements or criticisms of pages, products, concepts or whatever a page represents;
- XFN, used to represent human relationships;
- Rel-directory, to indicate that the destination of a link is a directory listing of files;
- Rel-enclosure, to indicate that the destination of a link is intended to be downloaded and cached;
- Rel-home, to indicate that the destination of a link is the homepage of a website.

These link-based microformats could be used to add machine-readable information to the so-called splash pages of institutional repositories. As an example, take Marvin Minsky's 'K-Lines: A Theory of Memory' article in MIT's institution repository. This is the webpage a human visitor would see when requesting a full record view of the article.

Search DSpace

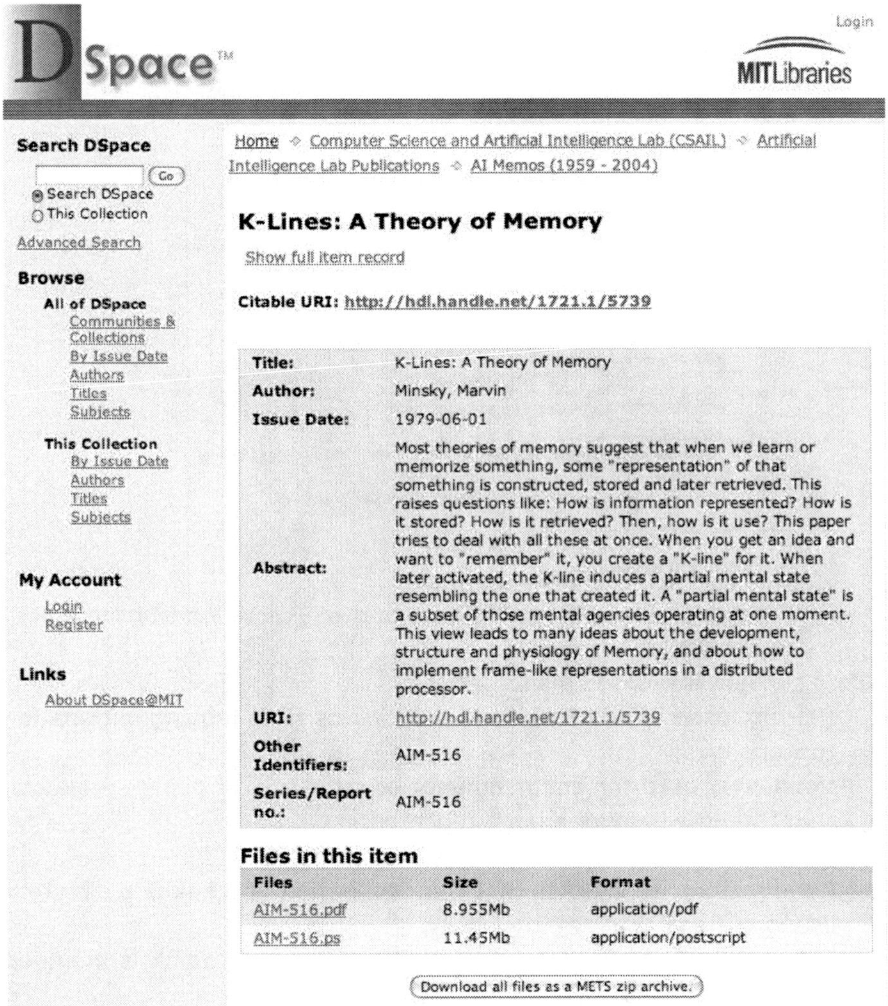

[   ] (Go)

◉ Search DSpace
○ This Collection

Advanced Search

Browse

All of DSpace
  Communities &
  Collections
  By Issue Date
  Authors
  Titles
  Subjects

This Collection
  By Issue Date
  Authors
  Titles
  Subjects

My Account
  Login
  Register

Links
  About DSpace@MIT

Home ◇ Computer Science and Artificial Intelligence Lab (CSAIL) ◇ Artificial Intelligence Lab Publications ◇ AI Memos (1959 - 2004)

K-Lines: A Theory of Memory

Show full item record

Citable URI: http://hdl.handle.net/1721.1/5739

Title:	K-Lines: A Theory of Memory
Author:	Minsky, Marvin
Issue Date:	1979-06-01
Abstract:	Most theories of memory suggest that when we learn or memorize something, some "representation" of that something is constructed, stored and later retrieved. This raises questions like: How is information represented? How is it stored? How is it retrieved? Then, how is it use? This paper tries to deal with all these at once. When you get an idea and want to "remember" it, you create a "K-line" for it. When later activated, the K-line induces a partial mental state resembling the one that created it. A "partial mental state" is a subset of those mental agencies operating at one moment. This view leads to many ideas about the development, structure and physiology of Memory, and about how to implement frame-like representations in a distributed processor.
URI:	http://hdl.handle.net/1721.1/5739
Other Identifiers:	AIM-516
Series/Report no.:	AIM-516

Files in this item

Files	Size	Format
AIM-516.pdf	8.955Mb	application/pdf
AIM-516.ps	11.45Mb	application/postscript

(Download all files as a METS zip archive.)

Figure 43. A DSpace splash page at MIT

To access the PDF or Postscript full text of the article, a human would click on the two links at the bottom of the page in figure 42. A machine, however, will find in HTML source code many links:

- Links to browse subparts of the collection;
- Links to login into the DSpace application;
- Links to the MIT homepage and DSpace software;
- Links to the page itself, using CNRI Handles;
- And, last but not least, links to the full-text versions of the article.

Without special guidance, it would not be easy for machines to download the correct data objects (Hochstenbach, 2008). This guidance could be introduced with help of microformats. If repository administrators would include a 'rel' attribute with value "enclosure" in every link to a downloadable file, then software agents scanning the web pages could discover these links and use them as input for applications such as Internet search engines. The same techniques used by Google and Yahoo to search for licensed material could be used to harvest and index the full text of open access publications.

The 'rel-enclosure' microformat is used by services such as FeedBurner (now acquired by Google) to scan blogs for downloadable content[159].

Complex Values

More complex annotations can be created using the structured HTML tags. One example is the XOXO microformat, which is used to produce simple outlines. XOXO enabled HTML documents show to human visitors nested lists of objects. Machines, however, when parsing a webpage in search for XOXO objects, could turn this nested list on-the-fly into a compound object ready for use in new services.

This HTML fragment provides a simple example:

```
<ol class="xoxo">
<li>Minsky, Marvin. K-Lines: A Theory of Memory
<ol>
<li><a
href="http://dspace.mit.edu/bitstream/1721.1/5739/2/AIM-
516.pdf">PDF version</a></li>
<li><a
href="http://dspace.mit.edu/bitstream/1721.1/5739/1/AIM-
516.ps">PostScript version</a></li>
</ol>
</li>
<li><a href="http://en.wikipedia.org/wiki/K-
line_(artificial_intelligence)">K-Line article in
Wikipedia</a></li>
</ol>
```

Figure 44. HTML fragment containing XOXO object

A human visitor to this webpage would see this:

---

[159] http://forums.feedburner.com/viewtopic.php?t=20 (last access on November 24th, 2008).

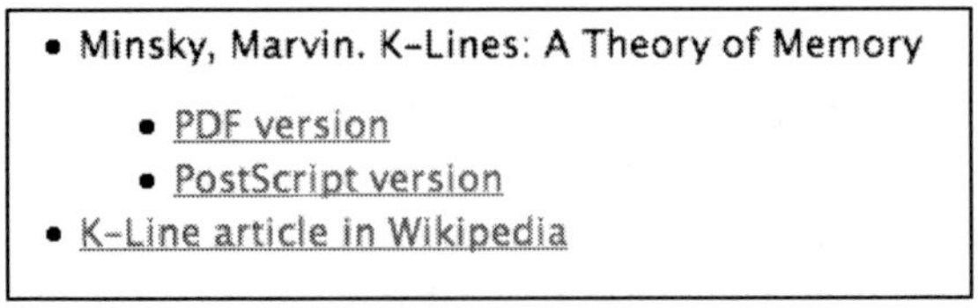

Figure 45. Sample rendering of XOXO document

A machine could parse this page, find the 'xoxo' outline and convert the HTML into a document that can be processed by METS, MPEG-21 or OAI-ORE applications.
Using structured HTML elements, microformats provide several specifications that are gaining popularity:
- XMDP, used to define metadata profiles that can be used to provide rich descriptions of web resources;
- hResume, used for publishing resumes and CVs;
- hAtom, used to transform WebPages into syndicated lists;
- COinS, used to embed OpenURL ContextObjects into web pages.

Formally, microformats are based on a combination of XHTML semantics with well-established Internet standards. For instance, the 'hCard' microformat uses XHTML semantics to provide the structure of the complex format, but the Internet standard RCF 2426 'vCard MIME Directory Profile' defines its values. Other examples are the combination of the 'geo' microformat for embedding geographic coordinates with the WGS84 specification for the World Geodetic System.

Microformats are gaining support from the W3C community that sees microformats as an important stepping-stone to the long-promised Semantic Web (Daly *et al.*, 2007). Standards such as GRDDL can be used to transform microformat annotated web pages into RDF documents. These RDF document can then be used to validate the annotations and create community-specific vocabularies by connecting microformat data with the Semantic Web tools such as RDFSchema and OWL (Gandon *et al.*, 2007).

An example of a microformat application in the world of digital scholarship is unAPI[160], a tiny HTTP API for the few basic operations necessary to copy discrete, identified content from any kind of web application.

---

[160] http://unapi.info (last access on November 24th, 2008).

There are already many APIs and protocols for syndicating, searching, harvesting and linking from diverse services on the web. They're widely used, but they're all different, for different reasons. unAPI only provides the few basic operations necessary to perform simple clipboard-like copy of content objects across all sites. It can be quickly implemented, consistently used, and easily layered over other well-known APIs.

8.2.2 Case Studies

The Zotero-Aquifer project experiments with microformats, e.g. coins, Hcards and unAPI. Thomas Habing from the University of Urbana-Champaign at Illinois works with Zotero in the Aquifer American Social History portal[161]. In this portal, they want to enable support for Zotero[162], browser-based (Firefox) software that enables researchers to manage, cite and collect references whilst surfing on the web. In the Aquifer project, microformats, especially unAPI, have proven them-selves a cheap and easy way to enable interoperability.

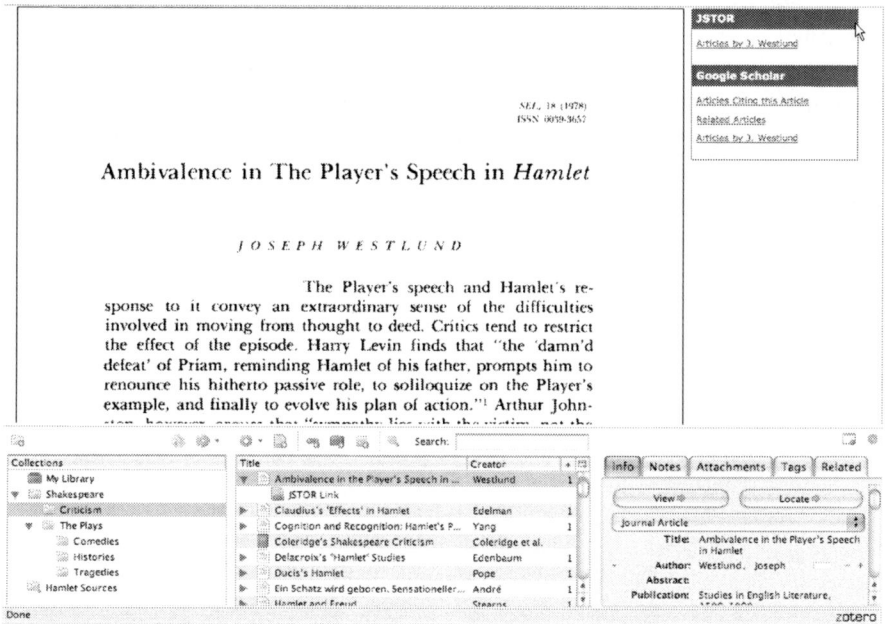

Figure 46. The Zotero software enables you to collect references and metadata through the browser (Taken from the Zotero demo video at
http://www.zotero.org/videos/tour/zotero_tour.htm, *on October 22nd, 2008)*

---

[161] http://www.dlfaquifer.org (last access on November 24th, 2008).

[162] http://dlfaquifer.blogspot.com/2007/09/zotero-integration-with-aquifer-portal.html (last access on November 24th, 2008).

According to Mr. Habing[163] from the project, microformats are more a philosophy than a specific technology. He also sees them growing more and more popular in the digital library community and in the Semantic Web community. Microformats seem to hold the promise of making the web more semantically friendly without requiring any major new infrastructure beyond http and html.

8.2.3 Opportunities for DRIVER

If DRIVER-users would also be Zotero users, then the use of microformats would be a great asset in terms of interoperability. Even when they don't use Zotero, microformats could be useful to present researchers with the possibility of collecting references they discover whilst working with DRIVER. It's possible that Zotero and other systems will support microformats in the future, and also, export to other bibliographic citation software systems would be useful for DRIVER. It is important for DRIVER to follow microformats developments as it allows for easy extraction of references from web pages. By editing the repository HTML page and adding semantic annotations as micro-formats, DRIVER harvesters would get machine readable access to binary content streams. The existing Dublin Core records could be used to expose the available publications, where following the DC:identifier link and parsing the resulting webpage for microformats would provide the data streams themselves.

---

[163] Personal e-mail communication on May 5th, 2008.

9. Old and New Publishing Formats

9.1. Introduction

'Open' publishing formats like ODF, OOXML, XHTML and MSXML are not new technologies. However, they do potentially offer a range of new opportunities for repositories. It may be possible to annotate publications to enable/improve, for example, extraction of references, descriptive metadata and links to external datasets. In this way Enhanced Publications can be semantically enriched and are crawlable by search engine spiders.

The two key international standards in this area, ODF and OOXML are described. As their 'packaging' features are already tackled this section will go into the markup components of these formats. As an example of a disciplinary application, CML is then reviewed. There are many other disciplinary examples, but chemistry provides an interesting scenario.

9.2 Open Document Format and Office Open XML

9.2.1 Open Document Format (ODF)

The OpenDocument format (ODF) is an open and free document file format for saving and exchanging editable office documents such as text documents, spreadsheets, databases, charts and presentations. It is intended to be an alternative to proprietary formats, including the commonly used DOC, XLS and PPT formats used by Microsoft Office and other applications. The specifications were originally developed by http://en.wikipedia.org/wiki/Sun_Microsystems. Sun, the standard, was developed by the OASIS industry consortium, based on the XML-based file format originally created by OpenOffice.org. It became an ISO standard, ISO/IEC 26300, in May 2006.

ODF is used in both free and proprietary software, by office suites, including OpenOffice.org, Google Docs, and individual applications. Microsoft has created the Open XML translator project to allow the conversion of documents between OOXML and ODF. In May 2008 Microsoft announced that Microsoft Office 2007 Service Pack 2 will add native support for ODF while, as already noted, support for OOXML will not be implemented until Microsoft Office 14[164].

Since one objective of open formats like OpenDocument is to guarantee long-term access to data without legal or technical barriers, some governments have come to view open formats as a public policy issue. For example in Germany, ODF is the standard that is recommended by the governmental office for standards in public IT and in Japan a new interoperability framework has been published which gives preference to the procurement of products that follow open standards including ODF.

9.2.2 Office Open XML (OOXML)

Office Open XML (OOXML) is a file format to represent spreadsheets, charts, presentation and word processing documents. An Office Open XML file may contain several documents encoded in specialised markup languages corresponding to applications within the Microsoft Office suite. Office Open XML defines multiple vocabularies using 27 namespaces and 89 schema modules.
The primary markup languages are:
* WordprocessingML for word-processing;
* SpreadsheetML for spreadsheets;
* PresentationML for presentations.

Shared markup language materials include:
* Office Math Markup Language, a mathematical markup language which can be embedded in WordprocessingML;
* DrawingML, a vector graphics markup language containing graphics effects such as shadows and reflection, mainly used in presentations created with PresentationML markup.

Custom XML schemas can also be used to extend Office Open XML. Office Open XML uses the Dublin Core Metadata Element Set and DCMI Metadata Terms to store document properties. There are some criticisms that OOXML has inconsistencies with existing ISO standards such as time and date formats, and that Office Math ML is used instead of MathML, which is recommended by W3C.

---

[164] http://en.wikipedia.org/wiki/Microsoft_Office_14 (last access on December 3rd, 2008).

9.2.3 Case Studies

Integrated Content Environment (ICE)

The Integrated Content Environment (ICE) is an open source content management system for academic material that takes word processing documents, from e.g. Microsoft Word or OpenOffice.org Writer, and turns them automatically into HTML and PDF. It can be used to in several ways:

- To manage documents for a small team or website;
- To build book-length courses for delivery online via the IMS packaging standard, and in print via PDF books;
- To write collaborative papers and conference presentations;
- To blog, using an Atom Publishing Protocol client implementation[165].

It has been developed at the University of Southern Queensland, a distance education specialist, and over 100 academic staff at USQ use ICE routinely for authoring their course material. Material can be repurposed as notes, lecturer's copies, slides, summaries etcetera, all managed through style sheets. Because the material is in XML, it is also possible to amend it with XML-aware tools or to generate new material through programming. A key aspect is that the structure of the document(s) can be managed in XML.

ODF is a key component within ICE since the conversion engine behind ICE uses OpenOffice.org as part of its transformation engine, and ODF is the OpenOffice.org Writer native format. However, users can work in either Microsoft Word or OpenOffice.org Writer. Given the debate between proponents of ODF and OOXML, the ICE approach is to use a subset of both formats, which is compatible and interoperable. ICE maintains detailed version control using the Subversion version control system, with an easy to use interface.

The project has also worked on embedding Chemical Markup Language (CML) into publications. It is possible to put a CML file into a working directory, and ICE will automatically turn it into a variety of formats. Similar services may be developed for other disciplines. A key aim of the project is to provide integration between the ICE content management system, which provides a repository for work in progress, and the ultimate destination in an institutional repository. ICE is

---

[165] http://ptsefton.com (last access on November 24th, 2008).

collaborating with the ARROW project and others in Australia to show how content can be ingested into Fedora and DSpace (Sefton, 2007).

ICE-TheOREM

There is also a project using ICE in the UK. JISC is funding the ICE-TheOREM project, which aims to demonstrate improved tool support for chemistry theses authoring and publication, using a range of available technologies including OAI-ORE. It will produce semantically rich HTML renditions of theses using ICE. It will also demonstrate integration between the ICE Thesis Management System and three repositories, EPrints, Fedora and DSpace. It uses ORE resource maps to describe the thesis and all its renditions. Examples are Word processing files in OOXML and/or ODF, HTML and PDF as well as chemical data, tabular data, and RDF.

9.2.4 Opportunities for DRIVER

Open formats such as ODF and OOXML enable services to open up access to structured content, as opposed to PDF, which can be reused by a range of other services, including aggregators such as DRIVER. Open formats also guarantee long-term accessibility. Given the ongoing controversy surrounding OOXML, an approach that is capable of using both ODF and OOXML, such as that adopted by ICE, is a sensible solution. There may be an increasing number of institutions using applications such as ICE that provide integration between systems which manage work in progress, and institutional repositories. DRIVER could potentially benefit from the increased access to scientific data and metadata made available as part of workflow processes. ICE is also using ORE resource maps, another indication of possible future relevancy for DRIVER.

9.3 CML

9.3.1 Theory

CML, or the Chemical Markup Language, was the first domain specific implementation based strictly on XML. Chemical information is traditionally stored in many different file types, which inhibit reuse of documents. CML uses XML's portability to help CML developers and chemists design interoperable documents[166]. Tools, schemes, documentation, mailing list, and links are available at Sourceforge[167].

CML is not a molecular markup language but is designed as a language for chemistry as a whole[168]. Components are reused, e.g. from MathML. Since it is a conformant XML language, any XML-conformant toolset can, in principle, interoperate with it. It is not simply 'another file format' but an expressive language in which a wide range of concepts can be constructed[169]. Elements of natural language are included. It is primarily aimed at communicating chemistry without semantic loss between systems that do not otherwise interoperate. These include:

- Humans to humans (e.g. authors to publishers);
- Humans to machines (e.g. job submission or ingestion of data);
- Machines to humans;
- Machines to machines (program to program).

As a result, complex semantic chains (workflows) can be built using XML as the transport layer. It separates ontology (meaning) from syntax and semantics by coupling concepts to dictionaries through the <tt>dictRef</tt> attribute. This allows groups of chemists and other scientists to build their own vocabularies. The three most active areas of CML usage at present are:

- Export and import from repositories or databases;
- Coupling processes in computational chemistry, e.g. input and output of large QM codes;
- Semantic publishing including the use of several markup languages like CML, MathML, SVG, and XSLT.

CML has been used by Peter Murray-Rust at the University of Cambridge to create a polymer building system and to represent Markush structures in a machine-processable way. It is also used to hold chemistry resulting from chemical natural language processing (OSCAR3), and to transform to and from RDF representations of molecules, substances and their properties.

---

[166] http://en.wikipedia.org/wiki/Chemical_Markup_Language (last access on November 24th, 2008).

[167] http://sourceforge.net/projects/cml (last access on November 24th, 2008).

[168] http://wwmm.ch.cam.ac.uk/blogs/cml/?p=27 (last access on November 24th, 2008).

[169] http://wwmm.ch.cam.ac.uk/blogs/cml/?p=26 (last access on November 24th, 2008).

CML uses standards wherever possible. It is based in SGML/XML and MIME; internally it uses ISO standards for dates and terminology[170]. JUMBO is a Java library that supports validation, reading and writing of CML as well as conversion of several legacy formats to CML. CMLSpect is an extension of CML for managing spectral and other analytical data (Kuhn *et al.*, 2007).

9.3.2 Case Study CrystalEye
The aim of the CrystalEye project is to aggregate crystallography from web resources, and to provide methods to easily browse, search, and to keep up to date with the latest published information[171].

There are thousands of crystal structures published in online journals every month. When an author has a structure published, they are obliged to provide the complete output of the structure elucidation experiment in the form of a CIF Crystallographic Information File (CIF) as supplementary material.

As this supplementary data is a set of facts and is not part of the full text of the article, it is not protected by copyright. CrystalEye has created a web spider, which 'listens' for new journal issues to be published and checks them for any CIF files. Upon finding a CIF file, it is downloaded and the data is passed through the processing part of the system. The work this performs includes converting the crystallographic data to CML. It also generates web pages for easy browsing of the data with 2D and 3D renderings of the structures.

At present the crystallography is being aggregated from the supplementary data to articles at publishers' websites. It is planned to extend this to aggregate from institutional repositories and also allow self-deposits. A major aspect of CrystalEye is the RSS feeds for current awareness, so the project is focusing on the latest journals in order for the CMLRSS to be tried out. A search facility is being added for retrospective data.

---

[170] http://www.ch.ic.ac.uk/omf/cml/doc/faq (last access on November 24th, 2008).

[171] http://wwmm.ch.cam.ac.uk/crystaleye/index.html (last access on November 24th, 2008).

9.3.3 Opportunities for DRIVER

It is likely that there are more domain-specific XML implementations such as CML becoming available. They may reuse existing interoperable XML components e.g. from MathML. These developments have the potential to make the aggregation of scientific data more straight-forward. There may also be opportunities for DRIVER to harvest from aggregators such as CrystalEye.

10. Web Services

10.1 Introduction

The world of web services is a very large subject area, almost impossible to describe and list exhaustively in a book. For that reason, the two largest subsets of web services, Resource-Oriented Architecture and Service-Oriented Architecture, are situated and for both is given a case study relevant to DRIVER: GData (ROA) and OKI (SOA). Interestingly, the DRIVER network itself uses a combination of SOA (for indexing and searching) and ROA (for the repositories).

10.2 Resource-oriented Architecture (ROA)

10.2.1 Theory
The concept of ROA is based on Thomas Fielding's Doctoral Thesis 'Architectural Styles and the Design of Network-based Software Architectures' (Fielding, 2000). It describes a web architecture that outlines how resources are defined and addressed using standard HTTP requests such as GET (retrieve a resource), PUT (ingest a resource), POST (update a resource) and DELETE (delete a resource). ROA is a subset of WOA, the Web-Oriented Architecture.

10.2.2 Case Study GData
GData[172] is a project by Google providing a simple standard protocol for reading and writing data on the web. GData uses either of two standard XML-based syndication formats: Atom or RSS. It also has a feed-publishing system that consists of the Atom publishing protocol plus some extensions, using Atom's standard extension model, for handling queries.

Feature	GData	Atom*	RSS 2.0
Syndication Format	Y	Y	Y
Queries	Y	N	N
Updates	Y	Y	N
Optimistic Concurrency	Y	N	N
Authentication	Y	N	N

10.2.3 Opportunities for DRIVER

GData is a widely used international protocol for delivery and archiving of data, and can be used by any individual, since it is a very easy way of dealing with data networks. It is an important example for DRIVER as a Grid structure for data. It is not SOAP-based and thus easier in use, which makes it so popular with a wide global user community. GData has a ROA-based architecture and is compatible with all Google's other applications such as Google Calendar, Google Base, Google Docs, etcetera. All these applications have a wide user community and many developers now use protocols similar to GData for their own applications, because the implementation is easier than SOA and more scalable for the Internet. Still SOA is also a good choice for DRIVER because it enables full control over which software packages will be part of the DRIVER node.

10.3 Service-oriented Architecture

10.3.1 Theory

SOA is an architecture mainly built to create interoperability between business processes. The aim is a loose coupling of systems and operating languages using protocols such as SOAP, WSDL, UDDI and a whole range of WS-related standards by OASIS[173]. Although SOA is built on Web standards, the services requested are defined by adding a new protocol layer instead of reusing the existing underlying architecture. Dr. M. Elkstein, author of 'LearnREST'[174], an online tutorial for Representational State Transfer (REST), gives a good indication of the differences between ROA and SOA:

> "The main advantage of SOA over ROA is the more mature tool support; however, this could change over time. Another SOA advantage includes the type-safety of XML requests. Developers can exactly define which messages need to be exchanged between different machines in the architecture."

---

[172] http://code.google.com/apis/gdata/overview.html#About (last access on November 24th, 2008).

[173] http://www.oasis-open.org/home/index.php (last access on November 24th, 2008).

[174] http://learn-rest.blogspot.com/2008/02/roa-vs-soa-rest-vs-soap.html (last access on November 24th, 2008).

The main advantage of ROA is ease of implementation, agility of the design, and the lightweight approach to things. In a way, SOA and SOAP are mainly used in the business world of tightly integrated intra- and extranets. Conversely, somebody that needs something up-and-running quickly, with good performance and low overhead, is often better off using REST and ROA. Rest and ROA are gaining popularity because of its easier deployment on a World Wide Web scale.

10.3.2 Case Study of Open Knowledge Initiative (OKI)

O.K.I.[175] (Open Knowledge Initiative) defines open architectural specifications that support the development of educational software by simplifying the methods of assembly, delivery and access to educational technology resources. The specifications comprise a service-oriented architecture based on high-level definitions.

10.3.3 Opportunities for DRIVER

The link with the e-learning community is important for DRIVER, since similar evolutions (Open courseware, ETDs) take place and the interoperability of both worlds is necessary for data exchange, and it benefits the ease of use for university library staff, faculty and students. OKI uses the SOAP protocol for external partners, and DRIVER uses SOAP internally, whereas it works more with ROA-type (Resource-Oriented Architecture) protocols for external partners. It is useful for DRIVER to keep watching the evolutions in web services such as OKI, especially when DRIVER would collaborate with partners from the industry later on. These mostly use SOAP-based applications. It is important for DRIVER to find the balance between the good and the bad sides of library and industry standards and stay compatible with both.

---

[175] http://www.okiproject.org (last access on November 24th, 2008).

References

1. On the Structure of this Book

Peters, D.; Schmidt, B. (2008) *European Network Plan.* Seventh Framework Programme Capacities. DRIVER II, Work Package 4, Deliverable 2.1.

2. GRID computing

Bégin, M.-E. (2008) *Summary report: "An EGEE comparative study: grids and clouds – evolution or revolution?".* EGEE. Presentation at OGF23, session: Exploring cloud computing.
http://www.ogf.org/OGF23/materials/1303/Grid+cloud+comparative+study+v1.ppt
(last access on November 20th, 2008).

Bégin, M.-E.; Jones, B.; Casey, J.; Laure, E.; Grey, F.; Loomis, C.; Kubli, R. (2008) *An EGEE comparative study: grids and clouds – evolution or revolution?* Members of EGEE-II Collaboration. EGEE-Grid-Cloud-v1.1.doc.
https://edms.cern.ch/file/925013/3/EGEE-Grid-Cloud.pdf
(last access on November 20th, 2008).

Foster, I.; Kishimoto, H.; Savva, A., eds. (2006) *The Open Grid Services Architecture.* Version 1.5. Open Grid Forum. GFD-I.080.
http://www.ogf.org/documents/GFD.80.pdf
(last access on November 20th, 2008).

Gentzsch, W. (2008) *Grids are Dead! Or are they?* Weblog at:
http://www.on-demandenterprise.com/features/26060699.html
(last access on November 20th, 2008).

Intel (2006) *Intel's Grid Programming Environment: an overview.* Intel Corporation White Paper.
http://gpe4gtk.sourceforge.net/GPE-Whitepaper.pdf
(last access on November 20th, 2008).

Jordan, C.; Kishimoto, H., eds. (2008) *Defining the Grid: a roadmap for OGSA® standards.* Version 1.1. Open Grid Forum. GFD-I.123.
http://www.ogf.org/documents/GFD.123.pdf
(last access on November 20th, 2008).

Snelling, D.F.; van den Berghe, S.; Li, V.Q. (2004) Explicit trust delegation: security for dynamic grids. *Fujitsu Sci. Tech. J.* 40 (2), 282-294.
http://www.unigrids.org/papers/explicittrust.pdf
(last access on November 20th, 2008).

Treadwell, J., ed. (2007) *Open Grid Services Architecture: glossary of terms*. Version 1.6. Open Grid Forum. GFD-I.120.
http://www.ogf.org/documents/GFD.120.pdf
(last access on November 20th, 2008).

Woutersen-Windhouwer S., R. Brandsma, Enhanced Publications: State of the Art. In: Vernooy-Gerritsen M. (ed), Enhanced Publications. Linking Publications and Research Data in Digital Repositories. SURF, Amsterdam University Press 2009

3. Current Research Information Systems (CRIS)

Baars, C.; Dijk, E.; Hogenaar, A.; van Meel, M. (2008) *Creating an Academic Information Domain: a Dutch example*. Paper presented at EuroCRIS 2008, Maribor, Slovenia, June 5th – 7th May 2008. pp. 77-87.
http://www.eurocris.org/fileadmin/Upload/Events/Conferences/CRIS200
8/Papers/cris2008_Baars_Dijk.pdf
(last access on November 21st, 2008).

Davis, P.M.; Connolly, M.J.L. (2007) Institutional repositories: Evaluating the reasons for non-use of Cornell University's installation of DSpace. *D-Lib Magazine* 13 (3/4).
http://www.dlib.org/dlib/march07/davis/03davis.html
(last access on November 21st, 2008).

ESF (2008) *Window to Science. Information Systems of European Research organisations.Report of the EUROHORCs –ESF Working Group on Joint Research Information System.* Strasbourg, European Science Foundation.
http://www.esf.org/publications.html
(last access on December 11th, 2008).

Feijen, M.; van der Kuil, A. (2005) A Recipe for Cream of Science: Special Content Recruitment for Dutch Institutional Repositories. *Ariadne* 45 (Oct).
http://www.ariadne.ac.uk/issue45/vanderkuil
(last access on November 21st, 2008).

Jeffery, K.G. (2000) An architecture for grey literature in a R&D context. *International Journal on Grey Literature* 1 (2), 64–72.

Jörg, B.; Jeffery, K.; Asserson, A.; van Grootel, G.; Grabczewski, E., eds. (2007) *CERIF2006-1.1 Full Data Model (FDM): model introduction and specification.* euroCRIS. CERIF 2006 FDM – Version 1.1.
http://www.dfki.de/~brigitte/CERIF/CERIF2006_1.1FDM/CERIF2006_FDM_1.1.pdf
(last access on November 21st, 2008).

Jörg, B.; Jeffery, K.; van Grootel, G.; Asserson, A.; Rasmussen, H.; Price, A.; Vestam, T.; Karstensen Elbaek, M.; Housos, N.; Voigt, R.; Simons, E.J., eds. (2008) *CERIF 2008 – 1.0: semantic layer specification for review.* euroCRIS. CERIF 2008 – 1.0 – Semantic Layer.
http://www.eurocris.org/fileadmin/Upload/CERIF/CERIF2008_1.0_SemanticLayer_forReview.pdf
(last access on November 21st, 2008).

Lagoze, C.; Van de Sompel, H. (2001) *The Open Archives Initiative: building a low-barrier interoperability framework.* Joint Conference on Digital Libraries 2001.
http://doi.ieeecomputersociety.org/10.1109/JCDL.2001.10061
http://www.openarchives.org/documents/jcdl2001-oai.pdf
(last access on November 21st, 2008).

Price, A. (2008) *A research information system as a research planning and evaluation tool: recent developments in Denmark.* International Conference on Current Research Information Systems, no. 9, Maribor Slovenia, pp. 173 – 182.
http://www.forskningsbase.life.ku.dk/fbspretrieve/8109615/CRIS2008_pricea.pdf
(last access on November 21st, 2008).

Razum, M.; Simons, E.; Horstmann, W. (2007) *Exchanging Research Information.* Institutional Repositories Workshop Strand Report, Knowledge Exchange, February 2007.
http://KE_IR_strand_report_Exchanging_Research_Information_Sept_07.pdf, downloadable from http://www.knowledge-exchange.info
(> Documents)
(last access on November 21st, 2008).

Rusbridge, C. (2008) *Repositories and the CRIS*. Posted on Digital Curration Blog 7. August 2008.
http://digitalcuration.blogspot.com/2008/08/repositories-and-cris.html
(last acces on November 21st, 2008).

Van der Graaf, M.; Van Eijndhoven (2008) *The European repository landscape: Inventory Study into the Present Type and Level of OAI-Compliant Digital repository Activities in the EU*. Amsterdam University Press.
http://dare.uva.nl/aup/nl/record/260225
(last access on December 10th, 2008).

4. Long-Term Preservation of Enhanced Publications

Abrams, S.; Morrissey, S.; Cramer, T. (2008) "What? So What?": the next-generation JHOVE2 architecture for format-aware characterisation. Paper presented at iPRES 2008: the Fifth International Conference on Preservation of Digital Objects, London, 29-30 September 2008.
http://www.bl.uk/ipres2008/programme.html.
See Consolidated Papers, http://www.bl.uk/ipres2008/ipres2008-proceedings.pdf pp. 96-102
(last access on November 22nd, 2008)

Ayris, P.; Davies, R.; McLeod, R.; Miao, R.; Shenton, H.; Wheatley, P. (2008) *The Life² final project report*. Research report. LIFE Project, London, UK.
http://eprints.ucl.ac.uk/11758/1/11758.pdf
(last access on November 22nd, 2008).

Beagrie, N.; Chruszcz, J.; Lavoie, B. (2008a) *Keeping research data safe: a cost model and guidance for UK universities*. Final Report, April 2008. HEFCE.
http://www.jisc.ac.uk/media/documents/publications/keepingresearchd atasafe0408.pdf
(last access on November 22nd, 2008).

Beagrie, N.; Semple, N.; Williams, P.; Wright, R. (2008b) *Digital preservation policies study, part 1: final report October 2008*. HEFCE.
http://www.jisc.ac.uk/media/documents/programmes/preservation/jisc policy_p1finalreport.pdf
(last access on November 22nd, 2008).

CASPAR (2007a) *CASPAR Overall Component Architecture and Component Model.* May 2007. CASPAR Consortium. Project no. 03357. CASPAR-D1301-TN-0101-1_1.
http://www.casparpreserves.eu/Members/cclrc/Deliverables/caspar-overall-component-architecture-and-component-model-1/at_download/file
(last access on November 22nd, 2008).

CASPAR (2007b) *CASPAR Conceptual Model - Phase 1.* May 2007. CASPAR Consortium. Project no. 033572. CASPAR-D1201-TN-0101-1_0.
http://www.casparpreserves.eu/Members/cclrc/Deliverables/caspar-conceptual-model-phase-1-1/at_download/file
(last access on November 22nd, 2008)

Digital Preservation Europe (2008) *DPE Repository Planning Checklist and Guidance DPED3.2.* HATII. Project no. 034762. IST-2006-034762.
http://www.digitalpreservationeurope.eu/publications/reports/Repository_Planning_Checklist_and_Guidance.pdf
(last access on November 22nd, 2008)

Guenther, R.S. (2008) Battle of the buzzwords: flexibility vs. interoperability when implementing PREMIS in METS. *D-Lib Magazine* 14 (7/8).
http://www.dlib.org/dlib/july08/guenther/07guenther.html
(last access on November 22nd, 2008).

Guidelines (2008) *Guidelines for using PREMIS with METS for exchange.* Revised June 25, 2008.
http://www.loc.gov/standards/premis/guidelines-premismets.pdf
(last access on November 22nd, 2008).

International Study (2008) *International study on the impact of copyright law on digital preservation.* A joint report of the Library of Congress National Digital Information Infrastructure and Preservation Program, the Joint Information Systems Committee, the Open Access to Knowledge (OAK) Law Project and the SURFFoundation. ISBN: 978-0-9802988-9-5.
http://www.digitalpreservation.gov/library/resources/pubs/docs/digital_preservation_final_report2008.pdf
(last access on November 22nd, 2008).

Jones, S.; Ross, S.; Ruusalepp, R.; Dobreva, M. (2008) *Data Audit Framework methodology*. Version 1.6. Draft for discussion. HATII.
http://www.data-audit.eu/DAF_Methodology.pdf
(last access on November 22nd, 2008).

Knight, G. (2008) *Framework for the definition of significant properties*. Report February 2008. InSPECT Project Document. wp33-propertiesreport-v1.doc.
http://www.significantproperties.org.uk/documents/wp33-propertiesreport-v1.pdf
(last access on November 22nd, 2008).

Lavoie, B.F. (2008) PREMIS with a fresh coat of paint: highlights from the revision of the PREMIS data dictionary for preservation metadata. *D-Lib Magazine* 14 (5/6).
http://www.dlib.org/dlib/may08/lavoie/05lavoie.html
(last access on November 22nd, 2008).

Lyon, L. (2007) Dealing with data: roles, rights, responsibilities and relationships. Consultancy report. UKOLN. data-consultancy-report-final.doc.
http://www.ukoln.ac.uk/ukoln/staff/e.j.lyon/reports/dealing_with_data_report-final.pdf
(last access on November 22nd, 2008).

PILIN Team (2007) *PILIN Project: project closure report*. Monash University.
https://www.pilin.net.au/Closure_Report.pdf
(last access on November 22nd, 2008).

PREMIS Editorial Committee (2008) *PREMIS data dictionary for preservation metadata*. Version 2.0. Library of Congress.
http://www.loc.gov/standards/premis/v2/premis-2-0.pdf
(last access on November 22nd, 2008).

Research Information Network (2008a) *Stewardship of digital research data: a framework of principles and guidelines: Responsibilities of research institutions and funders, data managers, learned societies and publishers*.
http://www.rin.ac.uk/files/Research%20Data%20Principles%20and%20Guidelines%20full%20version%20-%20final.pdf
(last access on November 22nd, 2008).

Research Information Network (2008b) *To share or not to share: publication and quality assurance of research data outputs: main report.* Report commissioned by the Research Information Network (RIN).
http://www.rin.ac.uk/files/Data%20publication%20report,%20main%20
0-%20final.pdf
(last access on November 22nd, 2008).

Rusbridge, C. (2008) *OAIS revision moving forward?.* Posted on Digital Curration Blog 8. September 2008.
http://digitalcuration.blogspot.com/2008/09/oais-revision-moving-
forward.html
(last access on November 22nd, 2008).

Sesink, L.; Harmsen, R.; van Horik, H., eds. (ca. 2008) *Data seal of approval: quality guidelines for digital research data in the Netherlands.* DANS.
http://DataSealofApproval.org.
http://datakeurmerk.nl.
http://www.datasealofapproval.org/files/datasealofapproval_1-
3_bw.pdf
(last access on November 22nd, 2008).

Sierman, B. (2007) Long-term preservation for institutional repositories. In: Weenink, K.; Waaijers, L.; van Godtsenhoven, K., eds. (2008) *A DRIVER's Guide to European Repositories: Five studies of important Digital Repository related issues and good Practices.* Amsterdam University Press, ISBN 9789053564110, pp. 153-184.
http://dare.uva.nl/aup/nl/record/260224
(last access on November 22nd, 2008).

Smith, M.; Moore, R.W. (2007) Digital archive policies and trusted digital repositories. International Journal of Digital Curation 2 (1), 92-101.
http://www.ijdc.net/ijdc/article/view/27/30
(last access on November 22nd, 2008).

UKRDS (2008) *The UK research data service feasibility study.* UKRDS Interim Report. Version v0.1a.030708. Serco Consulting.
http://www.ukrds.ac.uk/UKRDS%20SC%2010%20July%2008%20Item
%205%20(2).doc
(last access on November 22nd, 2008).

Verhaar P., Object Models and Functionalities. In: Vernooy-Gerritsen M. (ed), Enhanced Publications. Linking Publications and Research Data in Digital Repositories. SURF, Amsterdam University Press 2009

Watry, Paul (2007) Digital preservation theory and application: transcontinental persistent archives testbed activity. *International Journal of Digital Curation* 2 (2), 41-68.
http://www.ijdc.net/ijdc/article/view/43/50
(last access on November 22nd, 2008.)

Weenink, K.; Waaijers, L.; Van Godtsenhoven, K., eds. (2008) *A DRIVER's Guide to European Repositories: Five studies of important Digital Repository related issues and good practices.* Amsterdam University Press, ISBN 9789053564110.
http://dare.uva.nl/aup/nl/record/260224
(last access on November 22nd, 2008).

Woutersen-Windhouwer S., R. Brandsma, Enhanced Publications: State of the Art. In: Vernooy-Gerritsen M. (ed), Enhanced Publications. Linking Publications and Research Data in Digital Repositories. SURF, Amsterdam University Press 2009

5. Interoperability

Adida, B.; Birbeck, M.; McCarron, S.; Pemberton, S., eds. (2008) *RDFa in XHTML: syntax and processing: a collection of attributes and processing rules for extending XHTML to support RDF.* W3C recommendation 14 October 2008.
http://www.w3.org/TR/rdfa-syntax
(last access on November 24th, 2008).

Adobe (2005) *XMP™: adding intelligence to media.* XMP specification. San Jose, CA, Adobe Systems Incorporated.
http://www.adobe.com/devnet/xmp/pdfs/xmp_specification.pdf
(last access on November 23rd, 2008).

Allinson, J.; Johnston, P.; Powell, A. (2007) A Dublin Core application profile for scholarly works. *Ariadne* 50 (January).
http://www.ariadne.ac.uk/issue50/allinson-et-al
(last access on November 24th, 2008).

Allsopp, J. (2007) *Microformats: empowering your markup for Web 2.0.* New York, Springer Verlag. ISBN 1-59059-814-8

Bekaert, J.; Hochstenbach, P.; Van de Sompel, H. (2003) *Using MPEG-21 DIDL to represent complex digital objects in the Los Alamos National Laboratory Digital Library.* D-Lib Magazine 9 (11).
http://www.dlib.org/dlib/november03/bekaert/11bekaert.html
(last access on November 23rd, 2008).

Brauer, M.; Durusau, P.; Edwards, G.; Faure, D.; Magliery, T.; Vogelheim, D., eds. (2005) *Open Document Format for office applications (OpenDocument) v1.0.* OASIS Open. OASIS standard, 1 May 2005. OpenDocument-v1.0-os.sxw.
http://www.oasisopen.org/committees/download.php/12572/OpenDocument-v1.0-os.pdf
(last access on November 23rd, 2008).

Chavez, R.; Cole, T.W.; Dunn, J.; Foulonneau, M.; Habing, T.G.; Parod, W.; Staples, T. (2006) DLF-Aquifer asset actions experiment. *D-Lib Magazine* 12 (10).
http://www.dlib.org/dlib/october06/cole/10cole.html
(last access on November 24th, 2008).

Cheung, K.; Hunter, J. (2008) *The SCOPE system: Scientific Compound Object Publishing and Editing.* OAI-ORE Specification Roll-Out, Johns Hopkins University, Baltimore, MD USA, 3 March 2008.
http://www.openarchives.org/ore/meetings/hopkins/presentations/Hunter_ore.pdf (last access on November 24th, 2008).
A demonstration is available at http://www.openarchives.org/ore/
meetings/hopkins/presentations/SCOPE_demo.wmv
(last access on November 24th, 2008).

Cheung K, Hunter J, Lashtabeg A, Drennan J. (2007) *SCOPE: a Scientific Compound Object Publishing and Editing system.* 3rd International Digital Curation Conference, Washington DC, Dec 11-13, 2007.
http://www.itee.uq.edu.au/~eresearch/papers/2007/IDCC07.pdf
(last access on November 24th, 2008).

Cole, T.W. (2008) *OAI-ORE experiments at the University of Illinois Library at Urbana-Champaign.* OAI-ORE Specification Roll-Out, Johns Hopkins University, Baltimore, MD USA, 3 March 2008.
http://www.openarchives.org/ore/meetings/hopkins/presentations/Cole-OAI-ORE-Roll-Out.pdf
(last access on November 24th, 2008).

Consultative Committee for Space Data Systems (2002) *Reference model for an Open Archival Information System (AOIS)*. Washington, DC, CCSDS Secretariat. Blue Book, issue 1. CCSDS 650.0-B-1.
http://public.ccsds.org/publications/archive/650x0b1.pdf
(last access on November 23rd, 2008).

Daly, J.; Forgue, M.-C.; Hirakawa, Y. (2007) *W3C completes bridge between HTML/Microformats and Semantic Web: GRDDL gives web content hooks to powerful reuse and data integration.*
http://www.w3.org/2007/07/grddl-pressrelease.html.en
(last access on November 24th, 2008).

Deutsch, P. (1996) *RFC1951: DEFLATE Compressed Data Format Specification version 1.3*. Network Working Group.
http://www.faqs.org/rfcs/rfc1951.html
(last access on November 23rd, 2008).

DiLauro, T. (2008) *OAI-ORE fo publishing workflows: data archiving for journals of the American Astronomical Society*. OAI-ORE Specification Roll-Out, UK Open Day, University of Southampton, April 4, 2008.
http://www.openarchives.org/ore/meetings/Soton/
DiLauro-2008-04-04.pdf
(last access on November 24th, 2008).

Ditch, W. (2007) *XML-based office document standards*. HEFCE. JISC Technology and Standards Watch.
http://www.jisc.ac.uk/media/documents/techwatch/tsw0702pdf.pdf
(last access on November 24th, 2008).

Downing, J. (2008) *Preview of the TheOREM Project*. OAI-ORE Specification Roll-Out, UK Open Day, University of Southampton, April 4, 2008.
http://www.openarchives.org/ore/meetings/Soton/
TheOREM_Preview.pdf
(last access on November 24th, 2008).

Durusau, P.; Brauer, M.; Oppermann, L., eds. (2007) *Open Document Format for office applications (OpenDocument) v1.1*. OASIS Open. OASIS standard, 1 Feb. 2007. OpenDocument-v1.1-os.odt.
http://docs.oasis-open.org/office/v1.1/OS/OpenDocument-v1.1.pdf
(last access on November 23rd, 2008).

Eadie, M. (2008) Towards an application profile for images. *Ariadne* 55 (April). http://www.ariadne.ac.uk/issue55/eadie (last access on November 24th, 2008).

Fielding, R.T. (2000*) Architectural styles and the design of network-based software architectures.* University of California, Irvine. Dissertation. http://www.ics.uci.edu/~fielding/pubs/dissertation/top.htm (last access on November 24th, 2008).

Foulonneau, M.; André, F. (2008) *Investigative study of standards for digital repositories and related services.* Amsterdam University Press. ISBN 9789053564127. http://dare.uva.nl/document/93727 (last access on November 23rd, 2008).

Gandon, F.; Halpin, H.; Adida, B. (2007) *Bootstrapping the Semantic Web with GRDDL, Microformats, and RDFa.* INRIA. http://www.sop.inria.fr/acacia/personnel/Fabien.Gandon/tmp/grddl/grd dl-introduction-v3 (last access on November 24th, 2008).

Graham, M.J. (2008) *Portfolios: a framework for time-critical automated decisions.* OAI-ORE Specification Roll-Out, Johns Hopkins University, Baltimore, MD USA, 3 March 2008. http://www.openarchives.org/ore/meetings/hopkins/presentations/Matt hew_Graham_ORE.pdf (last access on November 24th, 2008).

Hickson, I.; Hyatt, D., eds. (2008) *HTML 5: a vocabulary and associated APIs for HTML and XHTML.* W3C working draft 10 June 2008. http://www.w3.org/TR/html5 (last access on November 24th, 2008).

Hochstenbach, P. (2008) *Understanding the OAI-ORE data model.* Posted on On digital Libraries, May 3, 2008. http://hochstenbach.wordpress.com/2008/05/03/understanding-the-oai-ore-data-model (last access on November 24th, 2008).

Institute of Electrical and Electronics Engineers (1990) *IEEE standard computer dictionary: a compilation of IEEE standard computer glossaries.* New York, NY.

Kuhn, S.; Helmus, T.; Lancashire, R.J.; Murray-Rust, P.; Rzepa, H.S.; Steinbeck, C.; Willighagen, E.L. (2007) Chemical markup, XML, and the World Wide Web, 7: CMLSpect, an XML vocabulary for spectral data. *Journal of Chemical Information and Modelling* 47 (6), 2015-2034

Lagoze, C.; Van de Sompel, H. (2007) *The OAI Object ReUse & Exchange (ORE) Initiative: report on work by the OAI-ORE Technical Committee.* Open Repositories 2007, San Antonio, January 25, 2007. http://www.openarchives.org/ore/documents/OR07.pdf (last access on November 24th, 2008).

Lagoze, C.; Van de Sompel, H.; Johnston, P.; Nelson, M.; Sanderson, R.; Warner, S., eds. (2008a) *ORE user guide: primer.* Open Archives Initiative Object Reuse and Exchange. Version 0.9. 11 July 2008. http://www.openarchives.org/ore/0.9/primer (last access on November 24th, 2008).

Lagoze, C.; Van de Sompel, H.; Johnston, P.; Nelson, M.; Sanderson, R.; Warner, S., eds. (2008b) *ORE user guide: primer.* Open Archives Initiative Object Reuse and Exchange. Version 1.0. 17 October 2008. http://www.openarchives.org/ore/1.0/primer (last access on November 24th, 2008).

Lagoze, C.; Van de Sompel, H.; Johnston, P.; Nelson, M.; Sanderson, R.; Warner, S., eds. (2008c) *ORE specification: abstract data model.* Open Archives Initiative Object Reuse and Exchange. Version 1.0. 17 October 2008. http://www.openarchives.org/ore/1.0/datamodel (last access on November 24th, 2008).

McGuinness, D.L.; van Harmelen, F., eds. (2004) *OWL Web Ontology Language: overview.* W3C recommendation 10 February 2004. http://www.w3.org/TR/owl-features (last access on November 24th, 2008).

Matthews, B.; Portwin, K.; Jones, C.; Lawrence, B. (2007) *Recommendations for data/publication linkage.* STFC, Rutherford Appleton Laboratory. CLADDIER Project Report III. http://claddier.badc.ac.uk/trac/raw-attachment/wiki/WikiStart/ Report_III_RecommendationsForDataLinking-final.doc (last access on November 24th, 2008).

Multimedia Description Schemes (MDS) Group (2005) *Introducing MPEG-21 DID: an overview.* International Organisation for Standardisation. ISO/IEC JTC 1/SC 29/WG 11/N7422.
http://www.chiariglione.org/MPEG/technologies/mp21-did/index.htm
(last access on November 23rd, 2008).

Nelson, M.L.; Koneru, S. (2008) *Client-side preservation techniques for ORE aggregations.* OAI-ORE Specification Roll-Out, UK Open Day, University of Southampton, April 4, 2008.
http://www.openarchives.org/ore/meetings/Soton/ore-amf-client-side-southampton.pdf
(last access on November 24th, 2008).

Nottingham, M.; Sayre, R., eds. (2005) *The Atom syndication format.* Network Working Group. RFC 4287.
http://www.ietf.org/rfc/rfc4287
(last access on November 23rd, 2008).

Sanderson, R.; Jones, R.; Llewellyn, C. (2008) *Functional object reuse and exchange: supporting information topology experiments.* OAI-ORE Specification Roll-Out, UK Open Day, University of Southampton, April 4, 2008.
http://www.openarchives.org/ore/meetings/Soton/foresite-ore_uk.pdf
(last access on November 24th, 2008).

Sefton, P. (2007) *An integrated approach to preparing, publishing, presenting and preserving theses.* 10th International Symposium on Electronic Theses and Dissertations, Uppsala, Sweden.
http://eprints.usq.edu.au/2653/1/Sefton_etd_2007.pdf
(last access on November 24th, 2008).

Smith, K.; Archer, P.; Perego, A., eds. (2008) *Protocol for Web Description Resources (POWDER): description resources.* W3C working draft 17 March 2008. http://www.w3.org/TR/2008/WD-powder-dr-20080317
(last access on November 24th, 2008).

Surface, T. (2003) *METS in the OCLC digital archive.* OCLC Online Computer Library Center (presentation).
http://www.loc.gov/standards/mets/presentations/surface.ppt
(last access on November 23rd, 2008).

Van de Sompel, H. (2008) *An introduction to the ORE interoperability framework*. 4th Search & Find Workshop, Ghent, Belgium, August 22, 2008.
http://public.lanl.gov/herbertv/presentations/ORE_Gent_hvds.pdf
(last access on November 24th, 2008).

Van de Sompel, H.; Nelson, M.L.; Lagoze, C.; Warner, S. (2004) Resource harvesting within the OAI-PMH framework. *D-Lib Magazine* 10 (12).
http://www.dlib.org/dlib/december04/vandesompel/
12vandesompel.html
(last access on November 23rd, 2008).

Verhaar P., Object Models and Functionalities. In: Vernooy-Gerritsen M. (ed), Enhanced Publications. Linking Publications and Research Data in Digital Repositories. SURF, Amsterdam University Press 2009

Verhoeven, H. (2006) *DIP interface specification*. IBM Nederland. Digital Information Archiving System.
http://kopal.langzeitarchivierung.de/downloads/kopal_DIAS_DIP_Interf
ace_Specification.pdf
(last access on November 23rd, 2008).

W3C HTML Working Group (2002) *XHTML^{TM} 1.0 the Extensible HyperText Markup Language: a reformulation of HTML 4 in XML 1.0*. Second edition. W3C recommendation 26 January 2000, revised 1 August 2002.
http://www.w3.org/TR/xhtml1
(last access on November 24th, 2008).

Weibel S. (2008) *Metadata: Semantics; Structure; Syntax*. Posted on Weibel Lines, February 18, 2008.
http://weibel-lines.typepad.com/weibelines/2008/02/metadata-
semant.html
(last access on November 23rd, 2008).

Lightning Source UK Ltd.
Milton Keynes UK
UKOW021500271011

181039UK00004B/7/P